Living Faiths

Christianity

Julie Haigh

Series Editor: Janet Dyson Consultant: Robert Bowie

OXFORD
UNIVERSITY PRESS

OXFORD
UNIVERSITY PRESS

Great Clarendon Street, Oxford OX2 6DP

Oxford University Press is a department of the University of Oxford. It furthers the University's objective of excellence in research, scholarship, and education by publishing worldwide in

Oxford   New York

Auckland   Cape Town   Dar es Salaam   Hong Kong   Karachi
Kuala Lumpur   Madrid   Melbourne   Mexico City   Nairobi
New Delhi   Shanghai   Taipei   Toronto

With offices in

Argentina   Austria   Brazil   Chile   Czech Republic   France   Greece
Guatemala   Hungary   Italy   Japan   Poland   Portugal   Singapore
South Korea   Switzerland   Thailand   Turkey   Ukraine   Vietnam

Oxford is a registered trade mark of Oxford University Press
in the UK and in certain other countries

British Library Cataloguing in Publication Data

Data available

ISBN-13: 978-0-19-913804-3

10 9 8 7 6 5 4 3 2 1

Printed by Bell & Bain Ltd, Glasgow

Acknowledgements
The publishers would like to thank the following for permissions to use their photographs:

Cover: Kate Kunac Tabinor/OUP; **p10**: GreenPimp/iStock; kadmy/iStock; shaunl/iStock; Vibrant Image Studio/Shutterstock; **p12** clockwise from top left: Maxx-Studio/Shutterstock; shutswis/Shutterstock; rangizzz/Shutterstock; kangshutters/Shutterstock; **p14**: Nancy Bauer/Shutterstock; **p16**: Pen Waggener/Getty; **p22**: vovan/Shutterstock; Gina Rothfels; Dinga; Joanne Harris and Daniel Bubnich; happydancing; Tomas Jasinskis; alicedaniel; Iwona Grodzka; Olga Kovalenko/Shutterstock; worker/Shutterstock; **p26tr**: TIM GRAHAM / Alamy; **p26b**: Flip Schulke/CORBIS; **p27**: Getty Images; **p28l**: Pascal Deloche/Godong/Corbis; **p28r**: Gideon Mendel/Corbis; **p29t**: Gary Roebuck/Alamy; **p31**: SuperStock/Getty; **p36**: SuperStock/Getty Images; **p37**: Dominic Lipinski/PA Archive/Press Association Images; **p40**: Adams Picture Library t/a apl/Alamy; **p41**: Bettmann/CORBIS; **p43**: Michele Falzone/Alamy; **p48**: Getty Images; **p49r**: Darren Baker/Shutterstock; **p51**: EDELMANN/SCIENCE PHOTO LIBRARY; **p52**: AFLO/AFLO/Nippon News/Corbis; **p53**: Petty Officer 1st class Shane T. McCoy/Reuters/Corbis; **p55**: ZUMA Wire Service/Alamy; **p56l**: REUTERS/Asmaa Waguih; **p56m**: AFP/Getty Images; **p56r**: david pearson/Alamy; **p57**: Getty Images; **p61**: Christine Langer-Pueschel/Shutterstock; **p64**: Gamma-Rapho via Getty Images; **p66**: Image Source/Getty Images; **p67**: Queerstock, Inc./Alamy; **p68tl**: Yuri Arcurs/

Shutterstock; **p68tr**: Flashon Studio/Shutterstock; **p70**: Design Pics Inc./Alamy; **p72t**: MS Bretherton/Alamy; **p72b**: Simon Rawles/Alamy; **p73**: Nick Turner/Alamy; **p74**: LondonPhotos/Alamy; **p74b**: pbyrne/Flickr; **p75**: Gamma-Rapho via Getty Images

Illustrations: Gareth Clarke

From the author, Julie Haigh: Many thanks to Janice Chan, Lois Durrant and Minh Ha Duong for their support and guidance. Thanks go also to Janet Dyson for her expert direction. Most of all, thanks to Dom and Maia Haigh for their continual love, support and endless cups of tea.

OUP wishes to thank the Arens, Feller and White families for agreeing to take part in the case study films and to be photographed for this title, and Meriel Carmen Colenutt and Chiara Ruggieri-Mitchell for being photographed for the cover. We would also like to thank Tim Gardner OP, Religious Education Adviser for the Catholic Education Service, Linda Foster, and Sue Collins, member of the Religious Society of Friends (Quakers) and retired school teacher, for reviewing this book.

We are grateful for permission to reprint extracts from the following copyright material:

The Holy Bible, New International Version®, NIV®, copyright © 1973, 1978, 1984, 2011 by Biblica Inc.™, reprinted by permission. All rights reserved worldwide.

The Archbishop's Council, Church of England for the traditional marriage vows of the Church of England.

The Religious Society of Friends (Quakers) for statement on marriage from www.quaker.org.uk.

Darrell Scott for transcript from you-tube post following the death of his daughter in the shootings at Columbine High School.

Although we have made every effort to trace and contact all copyright holders before publication this has not been possible in all cases. If notified, the publisher will rectify any errors or omissions at the earliest opportunity.

The websites recommended in this publication were correct at the time of going to press; however, websites may have been removed or web addresses changed since that time. OUP has made every attempt to suggest websites that are reliable and appropriate for students' use. It is not unknown for unscrupulous individuals to put unsuitable material on websites that may be accessed by students. Teachers should check all websites before allowing students to access them. OUP is not responsible for the content of external websites.

Contents

Introduction

What's it like to be a Christian?

The *Living Faiths* series helps you to learn about religion by meeting some young people and their families in the UK. Through the case studies in this book you will find out first-hand how their faith affects the way they live and the moral and ethical decisions they make. The big question you will explore is: What does it *mean* to be a Christian in twenty-first century Britain?

The icons indicate where you can actually hear and see young people sharing aspects of their daily lives through film, audio and music. This will help you to reflect on your own experiences, whether you belong to a religion or have a secular view of the world.

Key to icons

Image gallery   Audio   Film   Worksheet   Interactive Activity

The Student Book features

Starter activities get you thinking as soon as your lesson starts!

Activities are colour coded to identify three ways of exploring the rich diversity found within and between faiths. Through the questions and activities you will learn to:

- **think like a theologian**: these questions focus on understanding the nature of religious belief, its symbolism and spiritual significance
- **think like a philosopher**: these questions focus on analysing and debating ideas
- **think like a social scientist**: these questions focus on exploring and analysing why people do what they do and how belief affects action

You will be encouraged to think creatively and critically; to empathize, evaluate and respond to the views of others; to give reasons for your opinions and make connections; and draw conclusions.

Useful Words define the key terms, which appear in bold, to help you easily understand definitions. Meanings of words are also defined in the glossary.

Reflection

There will be time for you to reflect on what you've learned about the beliefs and practices of others and how they link to your own views.

Assessment

At the end of each chapter there is a final assessment task which helps you to show what you have learned.

Ways of helping you to assess your learning are part of every chapter:

- unit objectives set out what you will learn
- it's easy to see what standards you are aiming for using the 'I can' level statements
- you're encouraged to discuss and assess your own and each other's work
- you will feel confident in recognizing the next steps and how to improve.

We hope that you will enjoy reading and watching young people share their views, and that you will in turn gain the skills and knowledge to understand people with beliefs both similar to and different from your own.

Janet Dyson (Series Editor)   *Robert Bowie* (Series Consultant)

Meet the Families!

In this book, you will meet several young Christian families from across the UK. You can read about their thoughts and views on various topics covered in the book, and also watch their full interviews on the *Christianity Oxbox Online*.

The Arens family

Lilian and Richard live with their parents in Leicester. They go to Sunday services at Leicester Cathedral regularly and are very involved with the Anglican community. Mr Arens is a priest at the Cathedral, and both Lilian and Richard sing in cathedral choirs.

The Feller family lives in Oxford, and the children, Katie, Molly, Mikey and James, all go to a local Roman Catholic school. The family enjoys cycling and playing their instruments together.

The Feller family

The White family

Isaac White and his parents live in Oxford too. They are Quakers and attend Oxford's Friends' Meeting House, in the life of which they are very involved. When Isaac can drag his parents away from Quaker actions on social justice, the family enjoys listening to punk music and going to the cinema.

The origins of Christianity can be traced back to the birth of a Jewish boy named Jesus in Palestine over 2000 years ago who grew up to be a powerful and charismatic teacher. Some people saw him as the son of Joseph, an ordinary carpenter from Nazareth, and his wife Mary, but others, who understood his teachings and experienced his spiritual power, believed that he was Jesus Christ, the son of God.

The political and religious authorities of the time were challenged by the ideas and teachings of Jesus. At the age of 33 he was put on trial and condemned to death by crucifixion. Christians believe that after three days Jesus rose from the dead, an event known as 'the resurrection'. For Christians, this shows that Jesus has defeated death and they believe he continues to live in the lives of believers and the church as one of three aspects of God – the Father, the Son and the Holy Spirit – known as the Holy Trinity. Such beliefs can be difficult to understand, but the questions and activities in the books will make you think and help you explore some of these tricky theological and philosophical issues.

Many people would be surprised to know that Jesus was not a Christian – he was brought up to follow the Jewish religion. It was not until some years after his death that the followers of Jesus were given the name 'Christians' because of their belief that Jesus was Christ, the Son of God.

In the centuries after the death and resurrection of Jesus Christianity grew from small groups of believers who met in secret for fear of persecution to become the official religion of the Roman Empire. Today there are around 2.18 billion Christians around the world, and in the last census, 33 million people in the UK said they were Christians.

Since it began, Christianity has changed and developed in different ways and there have been disagreements about beliefs, practices and interpretations which have led to splits with the faith and, in some cases, even to wars. As a result, there are many different Christian groups or 'denominations' all under the wider umbrella of the Church. In this book you will meet members of several of these groups and find out what they believe, how they are different and how they practise their faith today.

Although they may do things differently, Christians share a common belief that Jesus is Jesus Christ, the Son of God, and that the Bible is the word of God. Worship plays an important part in the life of all Christians and they also all try to put the teachings of Jesus into practice in their daily lives. You will find that the Christians you meet in this book have different ways of worshipping and expressing their faith. They also have different ways of responding to life's big questions such as: 'Is it ever right to fight?', or 'Can science and religion agree?'. In this book you will have plenty of opportunities to discuss these questions and think about where you might stand on some of them. Enjoy the challenge!

Learning Objectives

In this unit you will:

- identify some features of Christian beliefs in God
- evaluate some Christian beliefs about the nature of God
- compare your beliefs with those of others.

- What do you think the dictionary definition of 'God' should be?
- Do you think there is 'anybody there'?

Case Study

The Feller family lives in Oxford. The Fellers are Roman Catholic Christians, who attend their local Catholic church and strongly believe in the existence of God.

Katie, the oldest child, says 'There is written evidence in the **Gospels** of the existence of God. He was a living man. There is a lot of written history about him'.

Mrs Feller believes that 'the most important thing about God is that you can always turn to him; he is always there. You can speak to him and ask him things'. She also finds that 'thinking about God is easiest when you are praying, singing, in church or taking part in **Mass**'. She says 'he is interested in everyone, because we are all part of him; he is over everything'.

James, the youngest, thinks that God is 'really, really powerful'. He says that 'God is easy to find when you are praying, because that is a language that God speaks'.

a Roman Catholics are Christians who believe the Pope is the head of the Church and who believe a Christian life includes taking part in Mass and other **sacraments**.

So where can God be found? If you look at some of the quotes from the Feller family on the opposite page, you can see where they look for evidence to support their belief in God – in the Bible, in the world around them, in places of worship, and through prayer.

Christians have offered other arguments to support their belief in God. An example is the idea that the world is so intricate and ordered that it cannot have happened by accident – it must have been created by God. People who don't believe in God would disagree with these arguments.

b Christians find God in many places, for example, in reading the Bible, in nature, at church or when praying.

Reflection

St Thomas Aquinas, a famous thirteenth-century Christian monk, said: 'Faith has to do with things that are not seen and hope with things that are not at hand'. Do you think you can believe in things that can't be seen?

Activities

1. Why might the idea that God 'was a living man' help Christians believe?
2. Write two sentences that compare your own thoughts about God with those of the Feller family. Discuss these with a partner.
3. What are the similarities and differences?

   Create a collage of images that illustrate Mrs Feller's belief that God is over everything and is always there.

1.2 Jesus: God or Man?

Learning Objectives

In this unit you will:

- explore what Christians believe about Jesus
- consider the concept of **salvation**
- reflect on the significance and role of the cross for believers.

Starter

- Do you know anything about Jesus? With a partner, see if you can fill a page with words or stories that you might have heard, e.g. Christmas.

The world is far from perfect. Christians believe the evil and suffering that exist in the world has come about because the relationship between God and humanity is broken. Christians believe that Jesus mends this relationship, and that Jesus was not just a man but was actually the Son of God, born on Earth in human form. The teachings of Jesus have been studied and passed on for about 2000 years since then.

Jesus has played an important part in human history, but people disagree about what Jesus the man was like. It can be assumed, according to accounts about him, that Jesus would have been Middle Eastern in appearance, because that was where he was born. His Jewish parents, Mary and Joseph, would also have raised him as a Jew.

born to Mary and Joseph
regularly visited the temple
raised by Mary and Joseph as a Jew
trained as a carpenter
baptised
chose 12 followers
taught crowds of people
went to Jerusalem for Passover
was arrested and put on trial
crucified
resurrected

a There are many different ideas about what Jesus would have been like.

? This diagram shows a simple overview of the life of Jesus according to the Bible, but many details of his life remain unknown. Discuss what you already know about each event and how Christians remember them.

Explore the role that Jesus' death and resurrection has had in the regular practices of the Christian Church in Unit 3.3.

After Jesus had been teaching for three years, he went to Jerusalem to celebrate **Passover** with his disciples. Here, he was betrayed by one of them, arrested, and put on trial under false accusations.

The Roman authorities sentenced Jesus to death by **crucifixion**, and he died on the day Christians call Good Friday. However, Christians believe he was **resurrected** on the day they call Easter Sunday.

Christians refer to Jesus as **Saviour** because his death put right everything that had broken down between God and humans. This means that humans are saved from sin without punishment, since Jesus himself took the punishment on the cross.

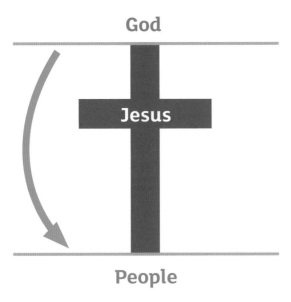

b This diagram represents the concept of salvation. Christians believe that Jesus' death brought humans closer to God.

Useful Words

Crucifixion A Roman method of execution that involved nailing a person to a large wooden cross until they died

Disciples Followers; Jesus had many disciples who he taught and lived among

Passover A Jewish festival celebrating the escape of the Jews from slavery

Resurrection The Christian belief that God raised Jesus from the dead on the third day after his crucifixion

Salvation Being saved from something; in Christianity, deliverance from sin and its consequences

Saviour A person or being who saves

Sins Things that people think, do, or don't do that go against what God wants

Reflection

Look at the image on the opposite page. Why do you think Christians picture Jesus in such different ways?

Activities

1. Go back to the work you did for the first Starter activity. Now add in all of the new words that you have learnt to describe Jesus.

2. Create a social networking post using no more than 140 characters, to explain why Jesus' crucifixion is important for Christians.

3. Imagine that you are a Christian who believes in salvation through the death and resurrection of Jesus. You are in charge of putting a Christian message in an advertising box on a website. Design the box, thinking carefully about what information you should include and who it is aimed at.

4. Does humanity need saving? Reflect on your answer and choose a format to present it in (a short speech, a written paragraph, or a visual display, for example).

1.3 Jesus: A Challenging Teacher

Learning Objectives

In this unit you will:

- examine some of Jesus' key teachings
- evaluate the impact of those teachings today
- reflect on how non-Christians might interpret Jesus' teachings.

Starter

- What in your life are you most attached to?
- Do you think we can be too attached to material things?

The Christian faith is based on the belief that Jesus was the Son of God, who came to Earth, was crucified and rose again. Some would argue that these are the most important claims about Jesus. However, it could also be argued that what he is thought to have taught, and how he taught it, is still hugely influential today – even for those who do not believe he was the Son of God.

According to the Bible, Jesus lived during a time when the Romans had great power and wealth. However, he spent most of his time with ordinary people, who worked hard for a living or needed some support. He was **controversial** because – unlike other religious leaders at the time – he chose to spend his time with those who were looked down on by society, such as **tax collectors** and the sick. (see Units 1.2 and 2.2)

> 'Do not store up for yourselves treasures on earth, where moth and rust destroy, and where thieves break in and steal. But store up for yourselves treasures in heaven […] For where your treasure is, there your heart will be also.'
>
> Matthew 6:19–21

? Read the above quotation. What do you think a 'treasure in heaven' is?

Useful Words

Controversial Likely to be opposed by many people

Tax collectors People who collect money for the Government (in Jesus' time, tax collectors were known for being corrupt)

a Some modern-day 'treasures on earth' might include cutting edge technology.

Jesus often challenged the big ideas of the time. For example, he thought that possessions could cause big problems and get in the way of finding God and living a good life.

Jesus thought it was better to choose the difficult rather than the easy path. He said it was always best to try to be faithful in relationships and that forgiveness was at the heart of human life, even though it was the hardest thing to do.

For Christians, and many others, his ideas are still revolutionary today.

Mark 10:17–22

Matthew 5:43–45

Mark 8:34–35

b These pictures represent very controversial teachings at the time of Jesus.

'To me, he was one of the greatest teachers humanity has ever had. To his believers, he was God's only begotten Son. Could the fact that I do or do not accept this belief make Jesus have any more or less influence in my life? Is all the grandeur of his teaching and of his doctrine to be forbidden to me? I cannot believe so.'

From the article 'What Jesus Means to Me' by Mahatma Gandhi (See Unit 4.5), published in the journal *The Modern Review* in 1941.

Reflection

Now that you know a little about what Jesus taught, would you be curious about listening to Jesus speak if he appeared tomorrow? Explain your response.

Activities

① See if you can put the Bible quotation into your own words. Is there more to life than owning things? Is it better to make friends with people who have lots of stuff? Explain your answers and what you think Jesus would say.

② Look up the Bible pasages in the artwork above.

  a Match the teachings with the images.

  b Identify what is controversial about each teaching.

  c How difficult do you think people would find each to do today?

d Read a bit more around these Bible passages. What else do they show about Jesus?

③ Look at the world around you and assess what status is given to possessions and wealth. Why might Jesus have the right to ask difficult questions about possessions and wealth?

④ Read Gandhi's quote on this page. Do you agree or disagree with him? Prepare a written or spoken response, making sure that you present a balanced argument.

1.4 How do Christians Understand the Holy Trinity?

Learning Objectives

In this unit you will:

- explore the idea of the **Holy Trinity** and its importance for Christians
- consider how the **Holy Spirit** helps Christians to understand something about God
- reflect on the many roles you play in your own life.

Starter

- How many things can you think of that work best in threes? For example, the three musketeers.

Christianity is a **monotheistic** faith – based on a belief in one God. However, the idea of the Holy Trinity, which is also central to Christianity, is more difficult to grasp.

The Trinity suggests that God exists in three persons:
- God the Father, who is the creator and the judge
- God the Son, the human, the teacher and the Saviour
- God the Holy Spirit, who is the guide and the comforter.

Christians believe that God the Father sent his Son, in the human form of Jesus, to teach and lead humans back to God. Jesus promised his disciples that after his death and resurrection, God would send the Holy Spirit.

'I will ask the Father, and he will give you another Counsellor to be with you for ever – the Spirit of truth [...] for he lives with you and will be in you.'
John 14:16–17

? Take some sticky notes or small bits of paper and write on each one a role you have in your life, for example, daughter/son, student, hockey player, singer, and so on. See how many you can come up with. Then, try to explain to a partner how one God could have three different roles.

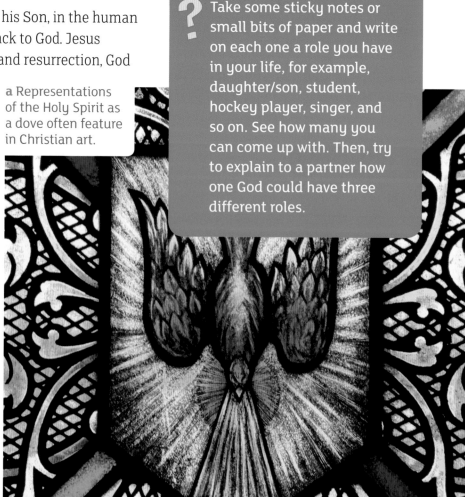

a Representations of the Holy Spirit as a dove often feature in Christian art.

Useful Words

Baptism A ceremony, involving the sprinkling of water, to welcome someone into the Church

Holy Trinity God in three persons: Father, Son and Holy Spirit

Holy Spirit The Spirit of God

Monotheism Belief in one God

Pentecost Originally a Jewish harvest festival; also the Christian celebration of the coming of the Holy Spirit to the disciples

Tongues A special language given by the Holy Spirit

The book of Acts (see the extract to the right) tells how the disciples were all together in a room in Jerusalem, celebrating the feast of **Pentecost** and wondering how they would find the courage to continue the work of Jesus. Jesus promised that the Holy Spirit would guide and comfort them.

Today, many Christians rely on the comfort and guidance of the Holy Spirit in their daily lives. Christians who belong to Pentecostal churches experience an 'outpouring' of the Holy Spirit that affects them physically. Some are inspired to speak in **tongues**, like the disciples. Other Christians describe their experience of the Holy Spirit as a calmness that comforts their soul, allowing them to focus on God. Some Christians believe the spirit empowers them in special ways at special times like **Baptism** (see Unit 1.5).

'Suddenly a sound like the blowing of a violent wind came from heaven and filled the whole house where they were sitting. They saw what seemed to be tongues of fire that separated and came to rest on each of them. All of them were filled with the Holy Spirit and began to speak in other tongues as the Spirit enabled them.'

Acts 2:2–4

Reflection

What animal or object would you choose to represent the idea of the Holy Spirit. Why?

b The Holy Spirit caused the diciples to speak in tongues.

Activities

1 Look back over the ideas in Units 1.1 to 1.3. What aspects of God are expressed through the Holy Spirit that are different from God the Father and God the Son?

2 Read the full story of Pentecost in Acts chapter 2. In pairs, prepare questions to ask either:
   a one of the disciples who experienced the Holy Spirit
   b or someone in the street who witnessed the event.

3 Prepare and present a two-minute report for the Jerusalem evening TV news highlighting the events of Pentecost.

4 Do some research to identify how the symbols of fire and a dove have been used to represent the Holy Spirit in Christian art. Use what you have discovered to help design a banner or a stained glass window to show the power of the Holy Spirit.

1.5 What does it Mean To Experience God?

Learning Objectives

In this unit you will:

- develop an understanding of what is meant by a 'religious experience'
- identify and analyse some ways in which Christians from different denominations believe they experience God
- evaluate the reasons given by people to explain how or why an experience is from God.

Starter

- What do you think a 'religious experience' is? Try to create a definition for it.
- Do you think it is possible to have a direct experience of God?

Case Study

As an Anglican priest, Mr Arens believes that it's possible to experience God day-to-day. He explains that his experiences are not as dramatic as those 'in Hollywood movies, where there is thunder and God speaks with a very deep Darth Vader voice'.

Mr Arens believes that one of the ways in which God communicates with him is when he creates 'space' for him. For Mr Arens, God can be felt or understood in times of silent thought.

However, he also believes that God can use others to communicate with him: 'We don't meet God just in silence, or through thunderous voices, but in other people. I do believe that God speaks to me through my community. It doesn't mean I enjoy it all the time, but I certainly experience God through them.' For him, communication with God is not always easy, but he believes that guidance helps him to become a better person.

> For me, it's important to make time for God. I am part of a community of people [...] we meet most days, pray together, and just make space for God in silence, which is a creative space to listen.

Useful Words

Anglican Part of the Church of England, the official Church of the country, with the Queen as head

Miracles Amazing events believed to be caused by God

Pentecostal churches Churches that have separated from the Roman Catholic Church and believe in the dramatic workings of the Holy Spirit

? Read what Mr Arens says about the ways in which he experiences God, and then summarize them in your own words. Choose two questions to ask him about his beliefs.

Case Study

Some Christians experience God in more dramatic ways. **Pentecostal churches** believe that God still does powerful things, as at Pentecost (See Unit 1.4). Christians who feel moved to express powerful feelings during worship link their experience to the Pentecost. Grace is a Christian who believes that she regularly experiences God in this way.

When I was growing up I heard some amazing things about Jesus, but I wasn't sure if he was really God. That all changed when I began to talk to him and asked him to show himself to me – he did! Now my relationship with God is the most important one in my life.

Often when I worship God, the Holy Spirit fills me with such a strong sense of the love of God that I feel physically, mentally and spiritually at peace. I talk to God about anything, and sometimes I use a different language, called tongues, which was given to me by the Holy Spirit to help me speak to God when I don't have the words. I've also experienced **miracles** – on several occasions God has physically healed me and others.

I've changed since I started following Jesus – I used to be quite fearful, but now I am more confident when faced with overwhelming situations.'

? Note down the different ways in which Grace experiences God. Then make a list of questions you would like to ask her if you met her in person.

Reflection

Have you ever had a dramatic life-changing experience? What happened? How did you feel?

Activities

1 Imagine if one of your friends told you that they had experienced God in one of the ways described in this unit. How would you react? Write a blog post describing what they said and how you felt.

2 Compare and contrast Grace's experience of God with Mr Arens' experience. What are the similarities and differences?

3 Using the ideas in this unit, design a stained-glass window, banner or bookmark to represent the workings of the Holy Spirit. Use shape and colour.

1.6 I Know I'm Unique but Why?

Learning Objectives

In this unit you will:

- analyse Biblical teachings that everyone is special to God
- explain the Quaker belief about the unique connection between humans and God
- identify what makes you unique.

Starter

- What makes people similar or different? Is it genes? Upbringing? Life experiences?

Christians believe that everyone is special and part of God's creation. The Bible teaches that human beings were made by God and are the pinnacle of his creation (see the quotation from Psalm 139). Throughout the **Old Testament**, God is described as caring deeply about each individual (see the quotation from Jeremiah). In the **New Testament**, Jesus taught about the worth of every individual to God (see the quotation from Luke).

a

'For you created my inmost being; you knit me together in my mother's womb.'
Psalm 139:13

'"For I know the plans I have for you," declared the Lord, "plans to prosper you and not to harm you, plans to give you hope and a future."'
Jeremiah 27:11

'Are not two sparrows sold for two pennies? Yet not one of them is forgotten by God. Indeed the very hairs of your head are numbered. Don't be afraid; you are worth more than many sparrows.'
Luke 12:7

? Read carefully through the three quotations and explain in your own words why Christians believe that all humans are special to God.

? Do you believe that you are unique, like every snowflake? What makes you unique? You could explain your answer with reference to song lyrics or quotes from books if you like.

So what do **Quakers** believe about the uniqueness of humanity? They often use the following quotation, adapted from the teachings of George Fox, the founder of Quakerism:

'*Walk cheerfully over the world answering that of God in everyone.*'

Case Study

Mr and Mrs White are Quakers who live near Oxford and who regularly attend meetings at the local Quaker Meeting House. Quakers believe that people are unique because they have something of God within them.

> The Quaker view is that there is that of God in everyone [...] God is **immanent** in the whole of creation, so we owe respect and reverence to the whole of creation.

> There is a great inward force of strength, of love, of wisdom, of creativity in every person.

Useful Words

Immanent God is present within his creation and his people
New Testament Collection of books and letters forming the second part of the Christian Bible
Old Testament Collection of books forming the first part of the Christian Bible, which is shared with Judaism
Quakers Members of the Religious Society of Friends, established by George Fox in the seventeenth centuary

Activities

1 Using any media you have access to, create a design for a Quaker poster to illustrate the idea that 'there is something of God in everyone'.

2 Choose five people in your life. What positive thing could you say about them that makes them unique?

3 What do you think it means when the Bible says that everyone is made in the image of God? Is this about our abilities, what we look like, or something else? Discuss this with a partner.

Reflection

What do you think Quakers mean when they say that there is something of God within every person? Compare this with the Hindu practice of 'Namaste' – showing respect to the Divine in human beings. What are the similarities and differences?

What do Christians Believe?

Objectives

- Explore and apply some key Christian beliefs about God.
- Reflect on your own ideas about God and the responsibilities you have in your life.

Task

'You gain nothing from a belief in God. There is no point believing.'

Do you agree or disagree? Your task is to produce a short, one minute speech. (Don't panic! Your teacher may only ask you to write it, not say it, but be ready just in case.) You need to decide whether or not you agree with the above statement. Then – using the ideas, arguments, concepts and tasks from this chapter – write a speech supporting or rejecting the statement.

A bit of guidance...

In order to convince the listener or reader that your choice (to support or reject the statement) is the correct one, you will need to include a few points from the opposing argument and show how they are weaker than your points. This will create a balanced argument.

Hints and tips

To help you tackle this task, you could refer to some of the following:

- Jesus, his example and his teachings
- God as creator and the source of all life
- The Holy Spirit as a guide and comfort
- Human beings as strong individuals

Think carefully about what points you will need to use for your speech. You could put them into speech bubbles in your book to help you get started.

Guidance

What level are you aiming at? Have a look at the grid below to see what you need to do to achieve that level. What would you need to do to improve your work?

	I can...
Level 3	• use religious vocabulary to describe some key features of the beliefs that Christians have about God • ask important questions about Christianity and beliefs about God, making links between my own responses and those of others.
Level 4	• use a range of religious vocabulary to describe and show understanding of the sources and beliefs that Christians have about God • raise, and suggest answers to questions about belonging, meaning, truth and commitment to a belief in God.
Level 5	• use a wide range of religious vocabulary to explain the impact of belief in God on individuals and communities, including Christians • ask and suggest answers to questions about belonging, meaning, truth and commitment to a belief in God, relating these to my own life and those of others.
Level 6	• use religious and philosophical language to give detailed accounts of belief and disbelief in God, explaining reasons for the differences between them • use arguments and examples to show the links between beliefs, teachings and experiences of a range of people, including Christians.

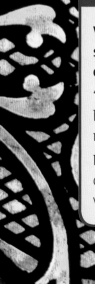

Ready for more?

When you have completed this task, you can also work on your skills for Levels 6 and 7, and perhaps even higher. This is an extension task.

'It has been argued that, even if God isn't real, there are many benefits to believing in something greater than us – because of the moral and social standards that belief can give people.'

Respond to this claim by showing how you could both agree and disagree with what it says. In order to attain the higher levels, you will need to evaluate relevant examples from life and the media.

2.1 God's Word or Ours?

Learning Objectives

In this unit you will:

- develop an understanding of what the Bible is
- consider the role of the Bible as a holy text for Christians
- evaluate the Christian idea that the Bible is the 'word of God'.

Starter

- If you could have a guidebook for your life written by just one person, who would it be and why? Discuss the reasons for your choice with a partner.

For Christians, the Bible is more than just a book. Many call it the 'word of God', because they believe that God inspired the human authors who wrote it.

Many people view the Bible as a guidebook for life, but many elements of it are often overlooked. The Bible is divided into two parts, the Old Testament and the New Testament (See Unit 1.6) and they contain many books by different authors, written in different styles. There are histories, law books, poetry, prophecy and letters, as well as the Gospels (which describe Jesus' life).

If someone were to make a film about what was in the Bible, it would end up with an 18 rating! There are stories about extreme violence with entire cities destroyed, humans eaten by wild animals, corrupt kings, books about love and sex, plus accounts of alcoholism and addiction. This is before you get to the brutal execution of Jesus and the vision of the destruction of the entire world at the end. This is the Bible, just not as you think you know it.

'All scripture is God-breathed'
2 Timothy 3:16a

? Think about the idea of words being 'God-breathed'. What do you think this means? Discuss with a partner.

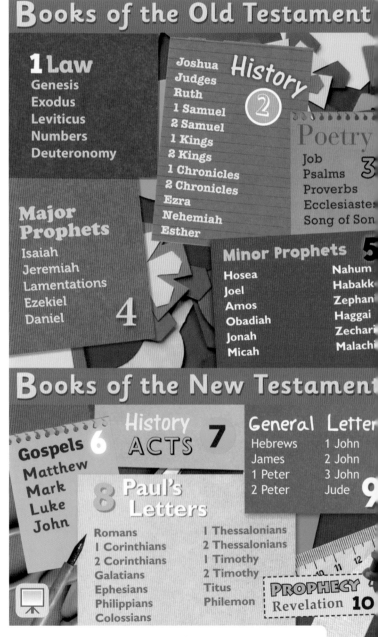

Books of the Old Testament

1 Law
Genesis
Exodus
Leviticus
Numbers
Deuteronomy

History ②
Joshua
Judges
Ruth
1 Samuel
2 Samuel
1 Kings
2 Kings
1 Chronicles
2 Chronicles
Ezra
Nehemiah
Esther

Poetry 3
Job
Psalms
Proverbs
Ecclesiastes
Song of Son...

Major Prophets
Isaiah
Jeremiah
Lamentations
Ezekiel
Daniel 4

Minor Prophets 5
Hosea
Joel
Amos
Obadiah
Jonah
Micah
Nahum
Habakk...
Zephan...
Haggai
Zechari...
Malachi

Books of the New Testament

Gospels 6
Matthew
Mark
Luke
John

History 7
ACTS

Paul's Letters 8
Romans
1 Corinthians
2 Corinthians
Galatians
Ephesians
Philippians
Colossians
1 Thessalonians
2 Thessalonians
1 Timothy
2 Timothy
Titus
Philemon

General Letter...
Hebrews
James
1 Peter
2 Peter
1 John
2 John
3 John
Jude 9

PROPHECY
Revelation 10

a The Bible was written by different authors over more than 2000 years.

So what role does the Bible have today? Well, for a believer, a very significant one. Many Christians believe that reading the Bible is one of the ways in which they can hear from God. For them, it is a document that provides guidance and comfort. They believe that many of its teachings can be applied to modern situations.

Others would argue that, because it was written so long ago, the Bible cannot possibly be relevant to their lives today. Many people might also question how accurately the Bible has been copied and translated into many different languages over the last 2000 years, and therefore how reliable it is as the 'word of God'.

Reflection

If you could have everything you needed for life written down in one book, what types of things do you think would be in it?

The Bible offers us nothing.

The Bible tells us a lot about the times in which its books were written but not much more.

There is much to learn from the Bible, and from other holy texts, but it is not the word of God, it's the word of wise people.

The Bible contains some truth and teachings from God, but some of it is out of date.

The Bible is the word of God; it is literally like God speaking to me.

? Read the statements in the speech bubbles and then put them in order, with the one you agree with most at the top. Explain your reasons.

Activities

① Using the information from this unit, create designs for the front covers of both the Old Testament ans the New Testament. Make notes around the edges giving reasons for your design choices.

② Look at several different Bibles, including some written for young children. What are some of the differences you see? What does this tell you about how these different Bibles are intended to be used?

③ 'The Bible is not the word of God, it was written by people.' With a partner, write down the arguments for and against this statement.

Learning Objectives

In this unit you will:

- learn what the New Testament is
- explain what the Gospels are and their importance for Christians today
- reflect on what you value in your own life.

- Work with a partner to mind-map the important events and stories in the life of Jesus.
- How did you get on? What else do you need to know to do this successfully?

The main source of information about the life and teachings of Jesus is the New Testament in the Bible. This is a collection of 27 early Christian writings, by different authors, mostly dating from the first century AD (the period after the death and resurrection of Jesus). Most of the information about Jesus can be found in the first four books – the Gospels – which were written after the death of Jesus by different Christian writers living in different communities. Gospel means 'good news' in Old English, and Christians believe that these four books tell the good news about Jesus.

The Gospels are titled according to who is believed to have written them (Matthew, Mark, Luke and John), and each of the writers tells Jesus' story from a different perspective. They are like four portraits, painted by four different artists. If you compare them, you will find many interesting differences – as well as many similarities. For example, Luke and Matthew both start with the birth of Jesus, whereas Mark and John begin with Jesus as an adult.

Useful Words

Priest An ordained person who leads a Christian community
Sermon/homily A talk given during a church service about a Bible passage or religious theme

? If your friends wrote your life story where would they begin? What key events would they include? What kind of person would their stories show you to be? Would the story be a 'true record' of your life?

a Why might portraits of the same person painted by different artists look completely different?

Case Study

The Feller family regularly listen to and use the Gospels in their worship. Their **priest** will read a story from the Gospels and base his **sermon/homily** on it, often making links to how it relates to modern life. The family will then reflect on the story by praying and thinking about how it can make a difference in their lives.

Katie explains how this works: 'Hearing stories about Jesus [and his teachings] prepares us for daily life. We can see how he has lived and then try to be the same.'

In one of the gospel stories, Jesus spoke to his disciples after watching a widow with barely any money still give away the last of what she had. All those around her had been giving large amounts that they could easily afford. Jesus said that, although the widow had given the least, it was more than all the others, because she 'out of her poverty, put in everything' (Mark 12: 41–44).

? How might Katie Feller try to apply the above story to her own life? What are the challenges?

Activities

1 **a** Look up each of the Gospel passages below and summarize what Jesus was saying in each case.
- Non-violent ways of solving conflict: Matthew 5:38–39; Matthew 5:43–45a
- Caring for the poor: Mark 14:7; Luke 6:20
- Getting on with other people: John 13:34–35; Luke 10:27

b Write down two ways each story might be interpreted.

2 How might a Christian put the teachings in Activity **1** into practice in their daily life today? How easy or difficult would it be to live like this?

3 Design a bookmark as a special present for Katie to use in her Bible; include words, pictures and symbols that reflect the way she values the Bible, particularly the Gospels.

Reflection

Many Christians value and read the Gospels more frequently than other books of the Bible, because they contain the life and example of Jesus. Do you have something you value more than anything else? If so, what is it and why is it so valuable to you?

2.3 How has Jesus Inspired Leaders?

Learning Objectives

In this unit you will:

- explore and apply the teachings of some Christian leaders
- identify ways in which leadership can strengthen faith or belief
- reflect on the qualities you would look for in a leader.

Starter

- Which people lead you in your life (parents, coaches, and so on)? How exactly do they do this?

The life of Jesus is an inspiration for Christian leaders. He set an example of how to lead others peacefully in a range of ways – by encouraging his disciples to pass on his message, by teaching crowds using stories, and by actively helping the poor and the sick. Many Christian leaders, like Martin Luther King Jr., have tried to follow Jesus' example. As a result, they have often made significant differences to people's lives.

Dr Martin Luther King Jr. (1929–1968) was a black American, born in a time of **segregation** in the southern United States. He became a **Baptist minister** and strongly believed that Jesus' example required a non-violent protest against oppression. He encouraged a large number of people to adopt this approach. He was a powerful leader in the **Civil Rights Movement**, which campaigned to end segregation and gain equal rights for black people, to whom King gave a strong, clear voice.

a

By blood, I am Albanian. By citizenship, an Indian. By faith, I am a Catholic nun. As to my calling, I belong entirely to the heart of Jesus.

? Mother Teresa of Calcutta was a famous Roman Catholic leader who won the Nobel Peace Prize in 1979. Do some research to find out how she was inspired by the life and teachings of Jesus.

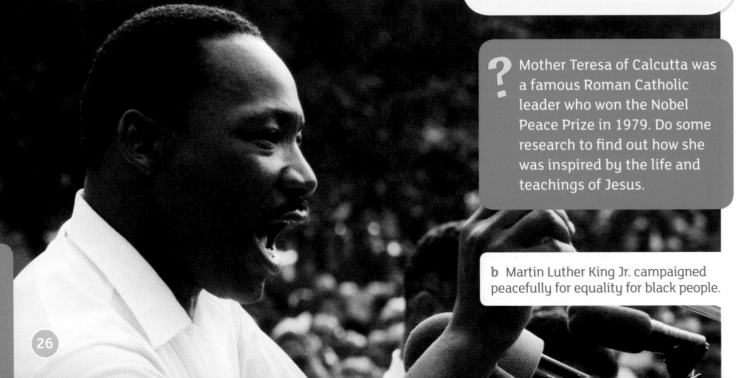

b Martin Luther King Jr. campaigned peacefully for equality for black people.

John Sentamu is the **Archbishop** of York. He was appointed to this position in 2005 and has spoken out about significant issues in Christianity, including the right to wear symbols of faith (such as the cross) in the workplace, and the freedom of a person to stand up for what they are proud of (see Unit 3.1).

Sentamu faced great prejudice when first appointed to his current position. He is considered by some Christians to act controversially at times. For example, he spent a week without food, camping in York Minster, in support of those suffering in the Middle East unrest. On live television, he removed and cut up his white clerical collar and vowed not to wear it again until the leader of Zimbabwe, Robert Mugabe, allowed all of his people to be free to have their own identities. Other Christians have argued that he stands alongside people in a profound way.

c Archbishop John Sentamu cut up his clerical collar on live television in an act of protest.

Useful Words

Archbishop A chief bishop responsible for a large area of the UK
Baptist A member of a Christian denomination that practises adult baptism
Civil Rights Movement A movement that fought for the rights of all people, regardless of their skin colour
Minister An ordained member of the Church
Segregation Legal and physical separation between black people and white people, especially in the southern USA up to the late 1960s

Reflection

If Dr King, Archbishop Sentamu and Jesus all met up in the twenty-first century, what do you think they might talk about?

Activities

1 Create a word cloud with all the characteristics that you think a good leader should have. You could use Dr King, Archbishop Sentamu and Mother Teresa as examples.

2 In pairs or threes, identify a cause that you think is worth at least raising your voice for. Create a storyboard for an online video to explain why people should pay attention to you and your cause.

3 Both Dr King and Archbishop Sentamu have followed Jesus' teachings about loving others and turning the other cheek. Find some of these

Gospel teachings and try to explain the impact that they might have had on these two men.

4 Discuss these three ideas with a partner and choose one to write about:

'We should be outraged by hate and inspired by kindness.'

'We should be free to express our beliefs.'

'We should live beside those who are suffering.'

Relate your thoughts and words to an issue or belief that is important to you.

Learning Objectives

In this unit you will:

- examine the many different ways in which people **worship**
- explore the value Christians place on worship
- consider the different approaches to worship in Christianity.

It has been estimated that there are 2.18 billion Christians in the world today. Within that number, there are many different Christian groups or **denominations** – all of which have different ways of expressing their Christian faith. While the underlying beliefs often remain the same, there can be big differences in the practices they adopt.

Christians show their love for God and their gratitude for Jesus' sacrifice in a number of ways, including coming together to worship, especially on a Sunday.

Useful Words

Denomination Different families of Churches, such as Catholic, Anglican and Pentecostal

Worship Any act that shows the devotion of the believer to God

Other Christians, such as Pentecostal Christians, worship in a more informal setting with more lively acts of worship, such as dancing, clapping and raising hands in the air.

Some Christians, such as Catholics, worship in quite a formal setting, with many of the community coming together on a Sunday. Roman Catholic worship tends to centre around the Mass, along with hymns and prayers.

Many churches, such as Anglican and Baptist churches, use a range of formal and informal worship in their services. There can be set prayers, or up-beat modern songs, depending on the church leader and the worshippers.

Case Study

Mr and Mrs White are Quakers – a denomination of Christianity that has built itself on the basis of little religious leadership, no set pattern for worship, and a practice of silence in meetings.

 Mrs White explains that 'Typically in a meeting for worship you might have about half an hour where it is silent, when people try to get rid of distracting thoughts. Then, you can reach a deeper place'. Anyone in the meeting may feel moved to speak during this time.

Reflection

'We worship things daily. Human life would be a little more dull without something to focus our attentions on.' Do you agree?

Activities

1. Compare and contrast the different types of worship.
   a. What actions can you identify?
   b. What differences do you think there are in the *atmosphere* of worship between these groups?

2. Discuss with a partner which of the ways of worshipping appeals to you the most. Why?

3. What is at the heart of worship for each of these Christian groups?

2.5 Is There Life After Death?

Learning Objectives

In this unit you will:

- develop an understanding of Christian teachings about life after death
- ask questions about why people have different beliefs about life after death
- reflect on the beliefs you may have about life after death.

Starter

- Complete these sentences:
  If heaven were ...
  ... a city it would be...
  ... a colour it would be...
- Now do the same for 'hell'.

Belief in life after death is at the heart of the Christian faith. Christians believe that – through his teachings, death and resurrection – Jesus showed that death is not the end.

The words spoken by Jesus to comfort his friend, Martha, after the death of her brother, Lazarus, are often recited at the beginning of Christian funerals, as the coffin is brought into the church (see the first quotation to the right).

In the Bible, the afterlife is often referred to as heaven or hell:

- Jesus described heaven to his disciples as being like a house (see the second quotation to the right). Many Christians believe that heaven is a place where they can go to be with God when they die, and that lots of people will be there.
- Jesus described hell as a place of destruction (see the third quotation to the right). Many Christians believe that heaven is where they can be with God, but hell is a place where God – and therefore goodness – is absent.

> *'I am the resurrection and the life. He who believes in me will live, even though he dies; and whoever lives and believes in me will never die.'*
> John 11:25–6

> *'Do not let your hearts be troubled [...] My Father's house has many rooms; if that were not so, would I have told you that I am going there to prepare a place for you?'*
> John 14:1–2

> *'Do not be afraid of those who kill the body but cannot kill the soul. Rather, be afraid of the one who can destroy both soul and body in hell.'*
> Matthew 10:28

? Create your own drawing or collage to consider the idea that heaven is like a house with many rooms.

There is a vast range of views amongst Christians about the afterlife. Some Christians believe that heaven and hell are physical places. They would say that heaven is a paradise where people who have followed Jesus are rewarded, and hell is a place of suffering and punishment for those who have not followed him.

Roman Catholics believe that after death, their journey continues towards God, but that because of the sins they have committed, they are not ready yet to experience God immediately. **Purgatory** is the place where people can be fully healed before they meet with God, and Roman Catholics continue to pray for those who have died, wishing them well on their journey into God's love.

Useful Words

Purgatory Mostly a Roman Catholic belief; a place or process where people who have died are healed fully (from their sins) before experiencing God in heaven

Reflection
Read the story of the crucifixion in Luke 23:32–43. What does the story tell Christians about life after death?

b This painting shows heaven, purgatory and hell.

Activities

1 Choose two beliefs about life after death from this unit and compare them with the beliefs of two other people in your class.

2 Read the following statements:
- 'There is more to life than the things we see.'
- 'This life is the only one we have – we need to make the best of it.'
- 'You reap what you sow.'

How would you respond to each point of view?

Which statement most closely reflects your own view?

3 'Hell is a scary idea to frighten people into doing good.'

'We are not perfect in life, so we need to be prepared to meet God in death.'

Choose one of these quotes to discuss with a partner and write about. Include what a Christian may think and what you feel about it.

How do Christians get to Heaven?

Learning Objectives

In this unit you will:

- consider a range of Christian beliefs about how people get to heaven
- evaluate the beliefs of Christians and ask questions about why they believe them
- reflect on whether or not a person's actions should affect what happens them after they die.

Starter

- Discuss with a partner:
  Have you ever …
  … been punished for something you've done wrong?
  … been let off the hook when you expected to get punished?

The Bible has a lot to say about heaven and hell, and creates a variety of impressions of both. While most Christians would agree that the afterlife exists, there is a huge range of views amongst Christians about how their life determines what happens when they die. For example, some Christians believe that they are guaranteed to go to heaven if they trust in Jesus.

Rachel is a member of a Free Church. She explains her views about God's grace and the afterlife below. The passage from Ephesians would support Rachel's views.

I believe that because we all do bad things, we all deserve punishment in hell. But the Bible says that Jesus took our punishment when he died on the cross, and that anyone who believes and trusts in him will go to heaven.

? Read Rachel's beliefs and the passage from Ephesians. What does it mean to be 'saved by grace'? Make a list of questions that you could ask Rachel which would clarify this.

'For it is by **grace** you have been saved, through faith—and this is not from yourselves, it is the gift of God—not by works, so that no one can boast.'
Ephesians 2:8–9

Some Christians would disagree with Rachel's views. They believe that the way in which they live their life will affect whether or not they get into heaven. For example, Lilian Arens believes that her day-to-day actions will impact on her afterlife.

Jesus tells a story in Matthew's Gospel about the afterlife (see the short extract below). The full story suggests that this decision will be made based on whether or not a person was kind to the needy during their lifetime.

? Read the full story in Matthew 25:31–46. Can you summarize what is happening? How might it support Lilian's view?

'I think if you have led a really bad life, and been a murderer or similar, then you go to hell. If you've lived a good life, then you go up to heaven to be with God'.

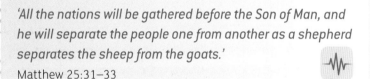

'All the nations will be gathered before the Son of Man, and he will separate the people one from another as a shepherd separates the sheep from the goats.'
Matthew 25:31–33

Useful Words

Grace God's love and blessing, given to all, even if they haven't earned it

Reflection

If there were a heaven, how would you decide who gets in and who doesn't?

I do hope that this is not everything. What form it will take I have absolutely no idea. [...] It is the heart of our faith that this life isn't everything and that this creation isn't finished. We live on the promise that God will sort it and finish it, and that is quite a wonderful thing.

Activities

1. Compare and contrast Rachel and Lilian's views in a table with the headings 'same' and 'different'. Why do you think they disagree about certain things?

2. Write key extracts from the Bible verses discussed in this unit in the middle of a piece of paper (Ephesians 2:8–9 and Matthew 25:31–46). With a partner, make notes around them on what they suggest a person needs to do to get to heaven. Are there any contradictions?

3. 'It's not possible to know anything about the afterlife, so why bother living a good life?' What might the people in this unit say in response to this statement? Write a short script of their conversation.

Where do Christian Beliefs Come From?

Objectives

- Explore, analyse and evaluate the different sources that Christians take their beliefs from.
- Explain common Christian beliefs.
- Identify and explain key differences in practice.

Task

Create a poster exploring the links between different sources of Christian beliefs, which could then be used as an instruction sheet by someone with no knowledge of where Christian beliefs come from. You will also need to show that you are familiar with common Christian beliefs and different Christian practices.

A bit of guidance...

You will need to carefully select ideas from each source (including the Bible, Christian leaders, worship and so on) and think of creative ways of presenting them. Give:

- a simple overview of the source
- reasons why it's accepted by some as a reliable source for belief
- reasons why its reliability could be challenged.

Then choose a way to present your findings in the poster, e.g. ICT, collage, newspaper-style, or another method of your choice.

Hints and tips

To help you tackle this task, you could refer to some of the following sources of authority for Christians:

- The Bible in general
- The Gospels in particular
- The example and teachings of Christian leaders like Dr Martin Luther King Jr. and Archbishop John Sentamu
- Religious experiences

You could also add a short reflection on your own life, and write about the books that are important to you, or leaders/teachers that you listen to and are inspired by. The sources you choose do not have to be religious ones.

Guidance

What level are you aiming at? Have a look at the grid below to see what you need to do to achieve that level. What would you need to do to improve your work?

	I can...
Level 3	• make links between beliefs and sources, including religious stories and sacred texts • identify what influences me, making links between aspects of my own and others' experiences.
Level 4	• show understanding of sources, practices, beliefs, ideas, feelings and experiences • raise and suggest answers to questions about belonging, meaning, truth and commitment to a belief in God.
Level 5	• explain how religious sources are used to provide answers to ultimate questions, recognising diversity in forms of religious expression • explain what inspires and influences me, expressing my and others' views on the challenges of belonging to a religion.
Level 6	• interpret sources and arguments, explaining the reasons why they are used in different ways by different traditions • use reasoning and examples to express insights into the relationship between beliefs, teachings, identity and belonging.

Ready for more?

When you have completed this task, you can also work on your skills for Levels 6 and 7, and perhaps even higher. This is an extension task.

Explain how you would respond to the following claim:

'Without authority and guidance we are nothing.'

This needs a written response that shows how you have worked through a number of different points. You will need to present arguments that both support and reject the quote, but you will also need to decide which side of the argument is stronger than the other. This decision will give you your conclusion. Make sure that your decision is based on the arguments you have presented.

3.1 Can I Show You Who I Am?

Learning Objectives

In this unit you will:

- explain the significance of some Christian symbols
- analyse the significance of symbols for individuals and groups
- discuss and evaluate whether people have the right to wear a religious symbol to work.

Starter

- Look around you. How many symbols do you see and what are they for?
- Name two Christian symbols. What do they mean?

Symbols are part of modern life. They represent many different things – from road directions to clothing companies. Many Christian symbols are very familiar (particularly the cross), whereas others are less familiar but just as significant for Christians. Roman Catholics have a number of symbols that play a part in prayer and worship.

Case Study

The Feller family has several Roman Catholic symbols at home, including a **crucifix** and a picture of the **Sacred Heart**. Mrs Feller believes that it's important to show people that they are Christians: 'It is a significant part of our lives and part of our culture; Christians shouldn't hide it, it is good to show it.'

a Jesus' heart represents his divine love for humanity

For some Roman Catholics, **rosary** beads enable them to pray, meditate and remember God in their daily lives. Katie Feller believes that the rosary helps her with her faith, because having a cross 'reminds us how Jesus laid down his life for us [without] thinking about himself.'

Mary, the mother of Jesus, is seen by Roman Catholics as a model for them to follow. The **Hail Mary** is recited 50 times as they pass the beads of the rosary through their fingers.

Case Study

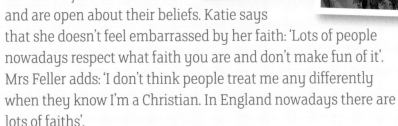

Can wearing religious symbols be a problem? Katie Feller and her mother don't think it's a problem for them and are open about their beliefs. Katie says that she doesn't feel embarrassed by her faith: 'Lots of people nowadays respect what faith you are and don't make fun of it'. Mrs Feller adds: 'I don't think people treat me any differently when they know I'm a Christian. In England nowadays there are lots of faiths'.

Useful Words

Crucifix The figure of Jesus nailed to a cross

Hail Mary A prayer to Mary the mother of Jesus, praising her and asking for her help

Rosary A string of beads with a cross, used in prayer and meditation

Sacred Heart A painting of Jesus showing his human heart, which symbolizes his love for humanity

Despite what Katie and her mother have experienced, there have been situations where other people have been challenged about displaying their faith at work, whether by wearing a cross or discussing prayer with colleagues. British Airways worker Nadia Eweida was banned from visibly wearing her cross when working on the British Airways check-in desk. There have also been negative consequences for others who have discussed or offered prayer for those in need around them. One of the reasons given has been that not everyone shares the same beliefs, and faith should therefore be expressed more privately.

? Do you think it matters if people like Nadia Eweida wear a religious symbol? Should it make a difference to anyone else? Give reasons for your answers.

Reflection

Would our modern lives work without signs and symbols? Which ones are essential?

Activities

1 a Imagine that you are Nadia Eweida, and your manager has asked you to remove your cross. Using your understanding of Christian beliefs, write an email from Nadia to British Airways explaining why you want to wear a cross on a regular basis.

b 'You are at work to do work. Your faith choices are irrelevant, so there should be no symbols allowed.' Come up with two more arguments like this one to support the decision made by British Airways.

c With a partner, role play the conversation that might take place between the opposing sides in this debate.

2 If you had a special object or a string of beads like a rosary to help you reflect, what or who would you want it to remind you of? Discuss your thoughts with a partner.

Learning Objectives

In this unit you will:

- develop an understanding of the role of community in Christianity
- examine links between belonging and Christian worship
- evaluate the ways in which you belong to a community.

Starter

- What makes a community? List the different ones you are a part of, then share and compare.

Being part of a community is important for people at all ages and stages of life, from toddler groups and friendship groups to sports teams and clubs. People join communities out of choice, or find themselves in one through school or work. They can provide identity, stability and a purpose in life.

Christians believe that they are all part of the 'body of Christ' – the wider Church across the world. Christians not only give time and commitment to their faith for themselves, they are also part of a supportive, extended family. Many churches meet regularly each week for Bible study and prayer, or to provide support groups. Christians see fellow believers in this wider community as vitally important.

> 'Now you are the body of Christ, and each one of you is a part of it.'
> 1 Corinthians 12:27

> 'The eye cannot say to the hand, "I don't need you!" And the head cannot say to the feet, "I don't need you!" On the contrary, those parts of the body that seem to be weaker are indispensable.'
> 1 Corinthians 12:21–2 and 26

? Where in your school or community can you find evidence to support these two quotations? Draw or write about it.

? Create a detailed dictionary definition for the phrase, 'the body of Christ', which explains what the phrase means and how it might be important to a Christian.

a Christians worldwide see themselves as being part of the larger 'body of Christ'.

Case Study

 Most Christians value worshipping with others, because they believe that God blesses them when they are together. They remember the words of Jesus: 'Where two or three come together in my name, I am there with them.' (Matthew 18:20)

Mr and Mrs White are Quakers, and they say that Quakers see themselves as not only part of the Quaker community, but also the wider Christian community. Although Quakers don't see particular days as more holy than others, Mrs White says 'Our roots are in Christianity. I will celebrate Christmas like other people who have a Christian heritage'.

Quakers worship in a plain, simple room in a 'meeting house'. They sit in silence, usually in a circle or square, and listen for God to move them. If they feel it's right, they will share their thoughts with the others in the meeting.

Mrs White points out that 'it does make a difference to sit in a meeting for worship with other people. I often feel that the people sitting in a circle together in silence creates a space that is hard to achieve on your own'. Mr White adds that 'one thing you can't get if you worship on your own in silence is that group exploration of an idea or experience'.

? Do you think that an individual could spend their time in solo worship, with no community worship at all? What would they gain or lose?

Reflection

Many Christians believe that worshipping together brings a real understanding of themselves and their faith. What shared activities do you love to do?

Activities

1. What do you think Jesus meant in the quote above from Matthew 18:20? How might Christians feel knowing that Jesus is present when they come together to worship?

2. Do you prefer to be on your own or in a group? Create a 'postcard' and explain your response on one side. Then illustrate your response on the other.

3. Go back to your answers from the starter activity. What responsibilities do you have as a member of the different communities on your list? What do you give and what do you take from them?

4. 'Community? What community? Everyone is out for themselves these days.' Using your own experiences, respond to this person using no more than 100 words.

3.3 Remembering and Celebrating

Learning Objectives

In this unit you will:

- learn the significance of the death of Jesus for Christians
- explain what the **Eucharist** is and why it is central to Christian belief and practice
- reflect on your own experiences of remembering and celebrating.

Starter

- What special events or memories in your life would you like to relive? How do you keep your memories alive?

Christians believe that the death of Jesus is the most important event in his life. It was the suffering and death of Jesus that made it possible for the resurrection to happen. Christians believe that Jesus was the son of God, and that God loved the world he had created so much that he was prepared to allow his son to die in order to save it. They believe that everyone is born sinful as a result of Adam and Eve having disobeyed God. This is known as Original Sin. By dying and rising from the dead, Jesus saved people from sin and enabled them to regain a close relationship with God. Read how John, a Gospel writer, describes this event in the quotation to the right.

> 'For God so loved the world that he gave his one and only Son, that whoever believes in him shall not perish but have eternal life.'
> John 3:16

? The theological ideas on this spread are difficult to understand. On a sticky note, write down something that puzzles you about the quotation and the information on these pages, something that interests you, and a question you would like to ask.

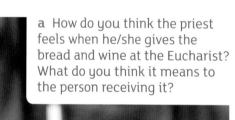

a How do you think the priest feels when he/she gives the bread and wine at the Eucharist? What do you think it means to the person receiving it?

Useful Words

Eucharist The meal of bread and wine that Christians share together to remember the death and resurrection of Jesus

Eucharist comes from the Greek word for 'thanksgiving'; Christians have different words for Eucharist – Roman Catholics call it Mass, and some Free Churches call it Holy Communion or The Lord's Supper; Quakers do not celebrate the Eucharist as they believe every meal should be treated as a sacrament.

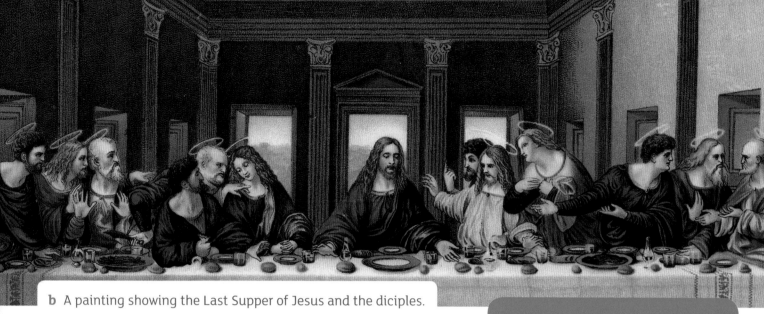

b A painting showing the Last Supper of Jesus and the diciples.

The night before he was crucified, Jesus shared a meal with his disciples, known as the Last Supper. While they were eating, Jesus shared bread and wine and said that they were his body and blood.

After the death of Jesus, two men were discussing the recent events with great sadness. They were joined by Jesus, although they didn't recognize him. Later, as they ate together, Jesus blessed and broke the bread and handed it to them. At that point, the two men recognized Jesus, but he had vanished. They were amazed, and told everyone they met about what had happened and how Jesus had become known to them when he broke the bread (see Luke 24:30–32).

Today, most Christians celebrate the Eucharist regularly to remind them of the death and resurrection of Jesus. The breaking of bread represents the breaking of Jesus' body, and the pouring of wine represents his blood that was shed.

> **?** Why do you think this ritual is so important to many Christians? Could they not just remember the death of Jesus without going through the ritual?

> *Reflection*
> Is there a meal or tradition that you share with family or friends? What do you repeat and why?

Activities

1 Design a poster to display on a church notice board explaining the significance of the Eucharist.

2 Prepare a role play or hot-seating activity where you question:
- one of the disciples after the Last Supper.
- one of the travellers on the road to Emmaus.

Prepare your questions or your role play carefully, paying attention to the details of the two stories.

3 Do some research to find out how some different Christian groups celebrate the Eucharist and write a brief report. What are the reasons for these differences? Share and discuss your findings.

3.4 Can it be Just Him and Me?

Learning Objectives

In this unit you will:

- explore the idea of private prayer
- critically examine the Christian belief that God communicates with humanity
- compare and contrast your beliefs with those of others.

Starter

- Why do you think people need one-to-one conversations? Draw an outline of a mobile phone and see if you can fill it with reasons.

Case Study

Christians believe that God is close to them and accessible to them at any time. They believe that their faith is not just about going to church or following certain rituals. It is often seen as a relationship between themselves and God – one that needs work and commitment. For many Christians, this is achieved through private worship. Lilian Arens says that she prays 'mostly every day [...] This is because I want God to talk to me'.

'I like to start the day with God and a cup of tea. I'll normally read a passage from the Bible and spend some time praying in silence or out loud. Sometimes I'll get my guitar out and sing a song to God. I'm the creative sort, so occasionally I'll write a prayer, or a poem, or the lyrics to a song. I also keep a journal of what I feel God's said to me, so that I don't forget.'

Phil and Jo are members of a Baptist church, and like to vary their times of worship.

? Compare these three examples of private prayer. In what ways are they similar and different?

'I don't have a fixed pattern for my time with God; I like to vary it, because I'm not very good at concentrating for a long time. I sometimes read the Bible or use some Bible reading notes to help me to understand what I'm reading. My favourite way to spend time with God is meeting up with some friends and praying with them about things that are happening in our lives.'

The belief that God is listening to you and wants a relationship with you, as if he is family, may seem strange to those who have not experienced it. Yet, Christians believe that God is their family – he is their Father and they are loved as his creation. If you look at what the different Christians featured in this book say about their faith, you will see that they express themselves as if God is a regular and familiar part of their lives. The artist Michelangelo, in his famous painting on the ceiling of the Sistine Chapel in the Vatican, shows Adam and God almost touching – as if they are a constant part of each other's lives.

a

? There are many questions to be asked about private prayer. Think of as many questions as you can. Draw round your own hands in your book and write your questions in the fingers.

b People work on their relationships with family and friends. Why not with God?

Reflection

If you had the chance to tell just one person how important they are to you, who would you choose and how would you tell them?

Activities

1 Create a definition of private prayer using around 15 words.

2 With a partner, look at the 'hands' you have filled with questions. Choose one of your partner's questions and try to answer it, giving your own opinion.

3 'Find out the meaning of the words, 'transcendent' and 'immanent' (not imminent) and then consider if it is possible for God to be both. Explain your decision to your partner and compare it with theirs.

4 'It is ridiculous to suggest that God can be a familiar part of an individual's life.' Create a flow chart that shows how you could respond to this statement, exploring a range of possible answers.

What is Lifelong Commitment?

Learning Objectives

In this unit you will:

- explain some ways in which Christians show commitment to their faith
- identify the stages that a Christian can go through in their beliefs
- reflect on what commitment might mean at different stages in your life.

Starter

- How many stages have you already been through in life (e.g. birth, walking, nursery)? Draw an outline of yourself and write them all inside it.

One of the main goals in Christianity is to be closer to God, and there are a number of ways that Christians express their commitment to this. The Catholic Church encourages younger members to take their **First Holy Communion**.

Katie Feller shares a photo of herself at her First Holy Communion.

This is me on my First Holy Communion day. I am wearing a white dress that symbolizes that I am pure and ready to take the Communion. The little prayer book is the book of prayers that I had learned.

Many parents choose for their young babies to be baptized (infant baptism), as a welcome into the Christian family. Others leave the choice up to their children, giving them the option to take part in believer's baptism when they are older.

? What questions would you ask Katie and Claire about their choices and experiences?

Claire goes to a church which practises believer's baptism: 'I was quite young when I got baptized, but I made the decision for myself. I knew that I wanted to publicly declare that my life was committed to following Jesus. When I was brought out of the water, it symbolized the start of a new life with him.'

Christians mark important stages in their faith with special ceremonies or **rites**. Mr and Mrs Arens explain how these happen in many Anglican churches, starting with babies.

Mr Arens says that 'the usual way of welcoming babies is by baptizing them. It's not only children [...] you can get baptized and confirmed at a later age'. He adds that in most Anglican churches 'baptism is with water and oil and it involves telling the child and the entire family that God loves that person, whatever they may do in their life'. Mrs Arens adds that 'it's also a symbol for the parents of the child that they have the support of the Christian **congregation**'.

Johannes also explains that the Anglican Church has a rite called **confirmation**. This is 'when teenagers or adults can say with their own words, "yes I want to be a Christian"'.

Reflection

Think about what commitments you might expect to make at different stages in your life. What signs, symbols and **rituals** might you choose to mark these commitments?

? Do you think that Christian parents should choose infant baptism for their child, or wait and let them choose when they are older?

Activities

1. Compare Claire's experience with the practices described by the Arens family. Note down the similarities and differences and discuss with a partner.

2. Research what is involved in being confirmed. Does it involve classes or taking a test? Do they have to wear anything special? Reflect on what you find and discuss with a partner how difficult or easy you think it would be for a young Christian to do.

3. Write an exchange of text messages or emails between Katie and Claire in which they explain the attractions of their different experiences.

4. Put together a Useful Words box for the words in **bold** in this unit. You may use the glossary to help you, but try to write in your own words.

Belonging to the Christian Faith

Objectives

- Evaluate and present your own responses to the ways in which a person expresses their Christian faith.
- Draw on examples from other faiths to compare and contrast a range of arguments linked to the right to express that faith.

Task

'Students and employees should be allowed to wear whatever religious symbols are significant to them. It is their religion.' Do you agree?

Using your learning from this chapter, you need to demonstrate that you have carefully considered the above statement and thought about both sides of the argument. You can choose, unless your teacher directs you otherwise, your method of recording this argument. It could be an essay, a letter, a speech, or a recorded film.

A bit of guidance...

Using Christianity as a starting point, it's important that you show understanding of the meaning behind different religious symbols and practices. This is a challenging question, because it's a topic that many people feel strongly about. Justify your points appropriately and give a fair amount of time to each side of the argument. Pay careful attention to the signifiance of symbols, sense of belonging, statement of faith, and commitment.

Hints and tips

The main focus for this assessment is on Christian symbols and practices, but you could refer to examples from other faiths, like the Muslim and Sikh examples included below, to develop your argument.

- Nadia Eweida was prevented from wearing a cross to work at British Airways (the example from Unit 3.1).
- In Luton, Icknield High School Muslim girls were banned from wearing headscarves.
- Sikh police officer, PC Gurmeal Singh was ordered to remove his turban when training.

Guidance

What level are you aiming at? Have a look at the grid below to see what you need to do to achieve that level. What would you need to do to improve your work?

	I can...
Level 3	• begin to identify the impact that religion has on believers' lives, and describe some forms of religious expression • ask important questions about expressions of belief, making links between my own responses and those of others.
Level 4	• describe the impact of religion on people's lives and suggest meanings for a range of religious expression • raise and suggest answers to questions about belonging, meaning, truth and commitment to a belief in God.
Level 5	• use a wide range of religious vocabulary to explain the impact of belief in God on individuals and communities, and describe why people belong to religions • ask and suggest answers to questions about belonging, meaning, truth and commitment to a belief in God, relating them to my own life and the lives of others.
Level 6	• explain why the impact of religions and beliefs on individuals, communities and societies varies • use arguments and examples to show the links between beliefs, teachings and experiences from a range of people, including Christians.

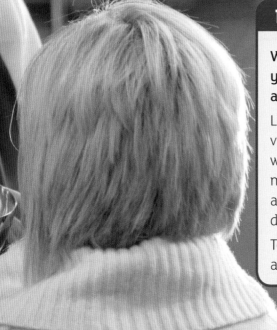

Ready for more?

When you have completed this task, you can also work on your skills for Levels 6 and 7, and perhaps even higher. This is an extension task.

Look at your school's uniform policy, and – depending on your viewpoint – write a letter as if to your school board of governors which outlines any changes or amendments that you would make. You might suggest that the uniform policy should include a statement about the importance of religious symbols in school dress, or an explanation about why this would be unacceptable.

To achieve the higher levels, you will need to present, support and justify your argument.

Learning Objectives

In this unit you will:

- critically examine the relationship between Christianity and science
- analyse some scientific and religious beliefs about the origins of the universe
- evaluate the roles played by science and religion in your life.

Science and religion are often thought to be in conflict. Faiths usually claim that a god is in control of the universe, whereas scientific theories about the origins of the universe are believed to contradict this.

However, Albert Einstein (a famous German-American physicist) said: 'Science without religion is lame, religion without science is blind.' So, despite their differences, Einstein felt that religion can give science meaning, and science can give religion strength. It is often said that science asks 'How?' and religion asks 'Why?' – both of which are extremely valuable questions.

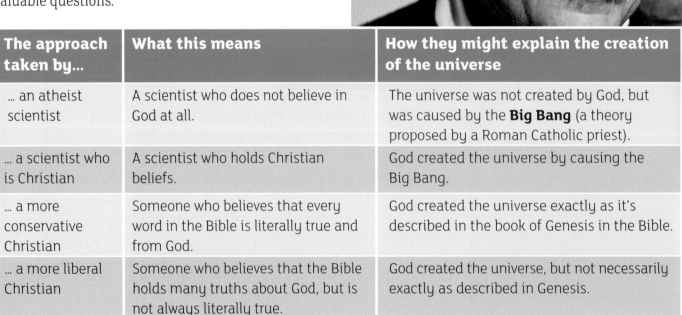

a Albert Einstein (1879–1955) developed the theory of relativity and wrote about the relationship between religion and science.

The approach taken by...	What this means	How they might explain the creation of the universe
... an atheist scientist	A scientist who does not believe in God at all.	The universe was not created by God, but was caused by the **Big Bang** (a theory proposed by a Roman Catholic priest).
... a scientist who is Christian	A scientist who holds Christian beliefs.	God created the universe by causing the Big Bang.
... a more conservative Christian	Someone who believes that every word in the Bible is literally true and from God.	God created the universe exactly as it's described in the book of Genesis in the Bible.
... a more liberal Christian	Someone who believes that the Bible holds many truths about God, but is not always literally true.	God created the universe, but not necessarily exactly as described in Genesis.

b The table above shows different ideas about the origins of the universe.

Many people have argued that the twenty-first century is the age of science, and that Christianity and other faiths have nothing more to give humanity. Some Christians have responded by saying that science is developing too fast – erasing the meaning in life that faith can provide. Some claim science is trying to explain away God.

Other Christians embrace the developments of science and celebrate the abilities that they believe God gave humans to explore and understand this world.

Useful Words

Big Bang A scientific theory that suggests the universe was created billions of years ago by an explosion of dense matter, which gradually expanded to form planets, stars – and eventually life itself, including humans

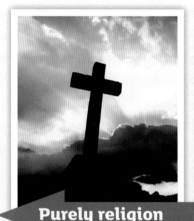

? Explain to a partner where you would put yourself on the continuum line below. Do you rely entirely on religion for your understanding of the universe, entirely on science, or somewhere in-between?

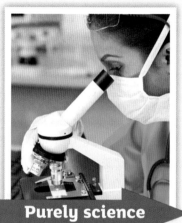

← Purely religion   **Purely science →**

? Read through Genesis 1 and 2 to see what the Bible says about the origins of the universe. Which of the approaches from the table would you adopt and why?

Reflection

Science: friend or foe? Explain your answer.

Activities

1 Imagine that you are God watching scientific knowledge develop in humans. Create a blog or a video that expresses your response to what you see.

2 How would you respond to Einstein's words? Write a postcard to the man himself explaining what you think.

3 In pairs, role-play a discussion between a more conservative Christian and a more liberal Christian, exploring their differing approaches to the origins of the universe. Use table **b** to help start your discussion.

4 'Science has killed off God.' Assume that this statement is correct, and that all religious belief disappears by 2025. Do you think the world will have changed from today? If so, how?

5 'If we could prove that God exists, we wouldn't be free to believe in him.' Discuss this statement with a partner.

Learning Objectives

In this unit you will:

- explain what is meant by the sanctity of life
- consider your view about when life begins and ends
- evaluate the role that faith can have in making life-changing decisions.

- Talk to a partner about how far you would go to protect the lives of your loved ones. Would you risk your own life?

Case Study

The Feller family follow the Roman Catholic teaching that all life is **sacred**. This means that they believe life is more valuable than anything else.

Mr and Mrs Feller explain that this belief impacts how they approach a number of issues, such as **abortion**. Mrs Feller believes that everything was made by God, so 'whether it be birds or ducks or humans, all life matters'.

The Roman Catholic Church teaches that abortion is wrong. It teaches that human life begins at **conception** right at the start of a pregnancy, so to end a pregnancy is to end a human life. However, Mrs Feller shares her personal view that 'sometimes in modern life you come up against great big barriers, whether it's because somebody's life is at risk, or the baby is so disabled that people feel it will be unfair on the child to carry on with the pregnancy'.

Mrs Feller believes that 'in an ideal world, no abortions should happen.' She doesn't think abortions shouldn't be made freely available for anybody and everybody, but she can see circumstances where women would feel enormous pressure.

'God [...] chose me even before I was born.'
(Galatians 1:15)

'If a man does not get his share of happiness [...] then I say a baby born dead is better. If it does that baby no good to be born [...] at least it found rest.'
(Ecclesiastes 6:3–5)

? Summarize the belief that 'all life is sacred'. Then think about the 'circumstances' referred to by Mrs Feller that might challenge this theory. What kinds of circumstances do you think she is referring to here?

A person's opinion about when life actually begins can have a significant impact on their views about abortion. Those who are described as being 'pro-life' might believe that life begins at the moment of conception. Others say that life doesn't begin until later in the pregnancy, so abortion is sometimes acceptable – but not after a certain point.

An alternative viewpoint is described as 'pro-choice'. Those who are pro-choice believe that the mother's rights are stronger than those of the **foetus**, so the mother has the right to choose to abort, regardless of when life begins.

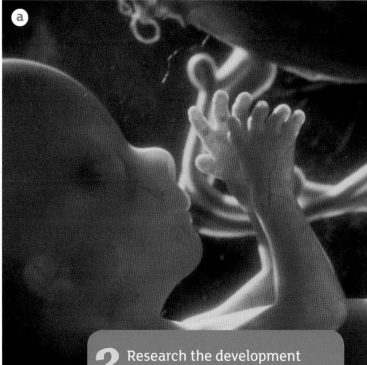

? Find out the main pro-life and pro-choice arguments, or come up with some yourself. Which arguments do you agree with most?

? Research the development of a human foetus from conception to birth. When do you think a human life actually begins? Explain in one sentence why you believe this, and then compare your thoughts with a partner.

Useful Words

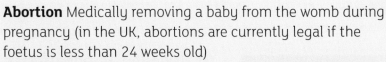

Abortion Medically removing a baby from the womb during pregnancy (in the UK, abortions are currently legal if the foetus is less than 24 weeks old)

Conception The moment that a sperm cell fertilizes an egg and a woman becomes pregnant

Foetus The name given to a developing human in pregnancy

Sacred Holy, unique

Reflection

Is all life sacred? Are there any forms of life or any humans for whom this doesn't apply?

Activities

1 Create a mind-map, collage or poem to explore the idea that 'life is sacred'.

2 a With a partner, role-play a discussion between a Christian who is pro-life and a Christian who is pro-choice. Try to draw upon your knowledge of Christian teachings to inform your debate.

b Write a short statement in response to the question: what part does faith play in making decisions about life and death?

3 'Life starts right at the beginning of a pregnancy. No one should end something that has started.' Do you agree? In small groups, produce a film, presentation or poster in response to this quote, using a range of views. You need to make sure that you give a balanced response, and also a clear conclusion that answers the question.

Learning Objectives

In this unit you will:

- explore and analyse what is meant by evil
- analyse theories about whether God and evil can exist at the same time
- evaluate explanations for the existence of evil.

The existence of 'evil' is a problem for people who believe in an all-loving God. Debates about this question have been going on for thousands of years.

Evil is often classified as one of two types:

- 'Natural evil' is the suffering caused by natural events, e.g. earthquakes or tsunamis (see photo below).
- 'Moral evil' is the suffering caused by other human beings, e.g. physical violence, murder or terrorism (see the photo opposite).

Christians recognize that it's hard to accept that God is all-loving and all-powerful when both natural and moral evil are allowed to exist.

'Do not be overcome by evil, but overcome evil with good.'
Romans 12:21

'Reject the wrong and choose the right.'
Isaiah 7:15

'Choose life, so that you and your children may live.'
Deuteronomy 30:19

? Create a collage of words, images or symbols to show the differences between natural evil and moral evil. Which one do you think is easier to accept?

a The aftermath of an earthquake that hit Japan in March 2011.

Christians have suggested many different arguments to explain why evil exists, such as these:

- The Devil (or **Satan**) exists, so a source of evil power exists on Earth.
- Evil has to exist to allow us to grow as humans, or as the consequence of **sin**. These two approaches are known as **theodicies**. The first was suggested by Irenaeus and the second by Augustine (both early Christian leaders). Irenaeus said that suffering allows us to get stronger and draw closer to God. Augustine said that suffering is the result of sin and turning our backs on God.
- Because **free will** exists, evil is always a possibility. By having free will, humans can choose either good or evil. Evil has to exist to allow humanity the freedom of choice.
- Evil is a mystery. All humans can do is cling to faith.

b Prisoners at Guantanamo Bay, which was infamous for the inhumane treatment some inmates received at the hands of the US military.

? Write down one of the arguments to the left in the centre of a large piece of paper. With a partner, or in threes, explore its strengths and weaknesses and then give it a mark out of ten for how convincing it is. You may want to do further research into the idea. Repeat this with the other arguments.

Useful Words

Free will Having the freedom to choose what to do

Satan In Christian belief, a supernatural person (or force) of evil in the world

Sin Something that people think, do, or don't do that goes against what God wants

Theodicy A theory that explains how God and evil coexist

Reflection

Is suffering worth what you may gain?

Activities

1. Using two sentences of roughly ten words each, explain natural and moral evil.

2. Assume that the reason evil exists is so that humanity can have free will. Would you give up your free will in order to never experience suffering? Explain your decision.

3. Discuss in pairs why each of you thinks evil and suffering exist. Then produce a role-play to show your decisions.

4. David Hume, an eighteenth-century philosopher, said that the existence of evil was the 'rock of atheism', meaning that it is a core proof of the non-existence of God. Using a collage, poem or mind-map, reflect on this idea.

Learning Objectives

In this unit you will:

- learn about the nature and challenges of forgiveness
- evaluate whether forgiveness is always possible
- interpret some biblical teachings about forgiveness
- reflect on your own views about forgiveness.

Starter

- Is there such a thing as an 'unforgivable act'?
- Think about the purposes of punishment. How many can you list?

Christians believe that Jesus died on the cross in order to bring forgiveness to anyone who asks for it. They believe that because of God's **grace** to them, Christians should show forgiveness to others.

Case Study

Many people find forgiving a hard thing to do, because human emotions – such as anger and a desire for revenge – can take over. Mr Arens preaches and teaches about forgiveness regularly, but even he still struggles with some aspects of it. He says that 'sin does matter and, if someone has done something absolutely horrible, I think forgiveness can just be cheap'.

'For if you forgive men when they sin against you, your heavenly Father will also forgive you. But if you do not forgive men their sins, your Father will not forgive your sins.'
Matthew 6:14–15

Christians believe that real forgiveness can take a long time and shouldn't be rushed. However, Mr Arens believes that, although it may be a difficult thing to do, it's important to forgive others with the help of God: 'What I am asked to do [...] is to pray for that person, and that does change things quite significantly'.

 Mr Arens explains that even those who are called to do God's work find forgiveness hard, but that – with prayer and understanding – this can change. Mrs Arens explains further: 'You might as well pray for yourself, for God to take your anger away [...] It's important not to retaliate and, in order to achieve that, it helps to pray for yourself and for the other person.'

Useful Words

Grace God's love and blessing, given to all, even if they haven't earned it

Case Study

Do you think you would be able to forgive the 'unforgivable'? Darrell Scott, a Christian, lost his daughter Rachel in 1999, when she was shot by two classmates at Columbine High School in the USA. The whole family was shattered and broken. Even so, Darrell and his family have forgiven the two gunmen and moved on to celebrate Rachel's life. Darrell explains below.

We made a choice to forgive and to celebrate Rachel's life. My daughter would not have wanted Eric and Dylan to ruin our lives because of unforgiveness. Forgiveness is something that we need to do over and over again until [...] the grace of God is firmly there for us to let go. For me personally, there is no way in my own strength I could have forgiven Eric and Dylan; I would have been mad at them for the rest of my life [...] I had to say "God I cannot forgive Eric and Dylan [...] but out of my weakness your strength is made perfect" [...] There is so much that opened up as a result of forgiveness.

Reflection

Does forgiving mean forgetting? Is it letting someone get away with something or is it about allowing you to move on?

Activities

1 Read the two case studies about forgiveness in this unit and explain in your own words why Christians believe that forgiveness is hard but necessary.

2 Using the Biblical quote on the left-hand page, write a radio interview with Mr Arens, Darrell Scott and Jesus. What would Jesus say to the two men and what would they say to him?

3 Think about where your strengths lie and produce a performance piece that explores your views on forgiveness. This could be a drama piece, a poem, a speech, a rap or a song; be imaginative.

4 'If one of my loved ones was killed, I would not forgive their killer.' Write a letter to Darrell Scott explaining whether you agree or disagree with this statement.

Learning Objectives

In this unit you will:

- explore why violence is used to solve conflict
- consider whether battles can be fought in another way
- develop an understanding about what a **pacifist** is
- evaluate the role of violence in Christianity and twenty-first-century living.

Starter

- Name as many wars or conflicts as you can.
- If the law said that all young people had to spend two years in the armed forces, would you be OK with that?

Is it ever right to fight? Many people believe that there are some situations where only the armed forces can make a difference – and some Christians agree with this, provided the war is a just war (see Unit 4.6). For example, if Britain hadn't responded with force to the threat of the Nazis in the Second World War, the world would be a very different place now. However, millions of people died fighting the Nazis, and some people believe that was a very high price to pay.

Other Christians see no reason for violence in any situation, and believe that only peaceful actions should be used to resolve conflict. These people are known as pacifists.

c

? Archbishop Desmond Tutu is a famous Christian pacifist. He was awarded the Nobel Peace Prize in 1984. Try to find out more about why he was given the Peace Prize. Do you agree with his words and actions?

a

b

? Colonel Gaddafi (former leader of Libya) and Saddam Hussein (former president of Iraq), both now deceased, were two modern dictators who were overthrown by the use of violence. If armed force had not been used, these two leaders might still be in power and using violence against their own people. Does using violence to end violence make sense?

Useful Words

Pacifist A person who believes in non-violent solutions to conflict

There are different approaches in the Bible towards violence and its necessity. The Old Testament contains many wars and battles. For example, Joshua fought to conquer the city of Jericho in the name of God (Joshua 6:20–21).

However, there is a greater emphasis on peace in the New Testament. Many modern Christians follow the example of Jesus, because he challenged many of the teachings in the Old Testament. One of Jesus' famous sayings is to 'turn the other cheek', which suggests that revenge and responding violently is unacceptable.

The threat of major violence and destruction, though, still convinces some Christians that violence can be necessary in certain situations provided that the principles of just war are followed.

'Resentment and anger are bad for your blood pressure and your digestion.'

'Do your little bit of good where you are; it's those little bits of good put together that overwhelm the world.'
Archbishop Desmond Tutu

? All of the British armed forces have Christian chaplains who aim to give spiritual guidance to those fighting in battle. The chaplains are serving members of the armed forces. Do you think they are allowed to wound or kill the enemy? Should they be? Make your decision and then find out if you are right.

d

Reflection

'We should all be pacifists, regardless of whether or not we have a faith.' Do you agree? Why or why not?

Activities

1. 'But if there is serious injury, you are to take life for life, eye for eye, tooth for tooth, [...] wound for wound, bruise for bruise.' (Exodus 21:23–25)
   'An eye for an eye makes the whole world blind.' (Mahatma Gandhi)
   Which do you agree with more – the Biblical verse or Gandhi's words?

2. One of the twentieth century's greatest leaders, and an inspiration for Martin Luther King (see Unit 2.3), was Mahatma Gandhi (see Units 4.2 and 5.5 in the *Hinduism Student Book*), who practised the Hindu principle of 'ahimsa'. Find out what ahimsa means and discuss how you think Gandhi would have responded to the situations described on this page.

3. Do a little bit of research and find more about the principles of 'just war'. Do you agree that it's OK to enter into violence if it's a just war?

Learning Objectives

In this unit you will:

- learn about the Quaker approach to conflict and war
- examine Christian teachings about peace and conflict
- consider whether or not there are times when pacifism cannot be maintained.

Starter

- Discuss the following statements with a partner: 'Loving your enemies is unrealistic in today's world.' 'Even if my family was threatened I would never fight back.'

Some Christians believe that the rejection of all violence is in line with the teachings of Jesus. Others believe that sometimes war is necessary, but that it must be fought in a way that satisfies certain moral principles – making it a **just war**.

The Society of Friends, or Quakers, began during the period of the English Civil Wars between King and Parliament (1642–1651). A group of men and women came together to find a way of living a Christian life that was simpler and more in line with the teachings of Jesus. They were also inspired by the teachings of George Fox (see Unit 1.6).

> 'I told them that I lived in the virtue of that life which took away the occasion for all wars.'
> George Fox (1624–1691)

Mr and Mrs White and their son Isaac are Quakers. They believe that living as pacifists is central to Quakerism. The Quaker Peace Testimony conveys the belief that the love and power of Jesus should be at the heart of all action, and that it is contrary to the spirit of Jesus to use war and violence. They believe that they should do everything they can to create a peaceful world.

> 'Blessed are the peacemakers, for they will be called the sons of God.'
> Matthew 5:9

> 'Love your enemies and pray for those who persecute you.'
> Matthew 5:44

For Quakers, being pacifists doesn't mean that they do nothing in a time of conflict. Mrs White explains that 'peace is an ongoing process, one that involves continual work'. She adds that 'many Quakers are involved in peace processes in many parts of the world'.

Quakers who became **conscientious objectors** in the First and Second World Wars refused to fight and were accused of being cowards by many in society. However, Mrs White says that many Quakers contributed in other ways by 'going onto the battlefield and rescuing wounded people'.

Useful Words

Conscientious objectors Those who refuse to fight on the grounds of religious beliefs or conscience
Just war The belief that wars can be morally justified if they meet certain criteria

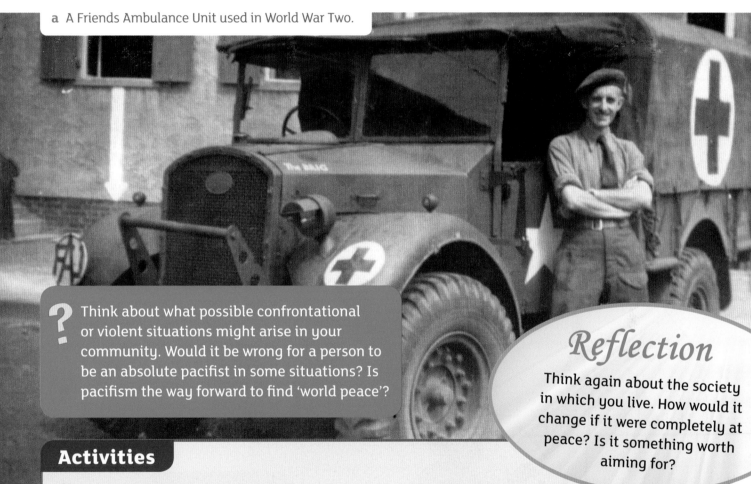

a A Friends Ambulance Unit used in World War Two.

? Think about what possible confrontational or violent situations might arise in your community. Would it be wrong for a person to be an absolute pacifist in some situations? Is pacifism the way forward to find 'world peace'?

Reflection

Think again about the society in which you live. How would it change if it were completely at peace? Is it something worth aiming for?

Activities

1 Create a car bumper sticker to explain why Quakers are pacifists.

2 Look at the quotations from Matthew.
   a Imagine that you were there when Jesus delivered these teachings. How do you feel? What questions do you want to ask him? Note down your thoughts and questions.
   b Choose three people who are likely to have an opinion about war (for example,

a Quaker, a soldier, a politician). Draw a speech bubble for each one that states how *they* would respond to Jesus' teachings.

3 'Peace is just a dream. It can never be a reality.' How would you respond to this? How would a Quaker respond to you? Write your response in a letter to the newspaper that has just published this statement.

4.7 Do Miracles Really Happen?

Learning Objectives

In this unit you will:

- develop an understanding of some different definitions of a miracle
- consider whether or not a miracle is possible today
- evaluate the Christian view of miracles.

Starter

- With a partner, define 'miracle'.

- Do you think it's possible for an event to be called a miracle? Why or why not?

At the heart of the Christian faith is the miracle of Jesus' resurrection. Many Christians believe that God, by his very nature, is a miracle maker.

The Bible describes miracles taking place both during Jesus' lifetime and after his death. Jesus healed the blind and the lame, calmed storms and brought people back from the dead.

'As Jesus approached Jericho, a blind man was sitting by the roadside begging. When he heard the crowd going by, he asked what was happening. They told him "Jesus of Nazareth is passing by." He called out "Jesus, Son of David, have mercy on me!" […] Jesus stopped and ordered the man to be brought to him. When he came near, Jesus asked him "What do you want me to do for you?" "Lord, I want to see", he replied. Jesus said to him "Receive your sight; your faith has healed you." Immediately he received his sight and followed Jesus, praising God.'

Luke 18:35–43

? Read the story above carefully. If you heard about an event like this in the news today, what would your reaction be? How do you think a modern Christian would react? Using your answers, write a script for a newsreader reporting the event.

Case Study

Some Christians believe God can do miraculous things today which can't be explained by science. Others think God works through science to do miraculous things.

Mrs Arens says that she doesn't think it's important to believe that things happened exactly as they are described in the Bible. She says she focuses on the fact that 'God has done something and has turned things around'.

Mr Arens says that he tries to 'keep an open mind' about miracles. However, he adds that he's experienced other, more subtle, miraculous occurrences: 'I believe that if somebody recovers from alcoholism, stops drinking and turns their life around through spirituality, then that – for me – is something miraculous, and I've seen that happen.'

Reflection

'Life itself is a miracle. Celebrate it.' Do we need to look any further than this?

There is a church in Northern Ireland which believes that God can heal people today. I heard about this in my church and we decided to see it for ourselves. My friend Holly had a very painful back at the time. It turned out that her legs were different lengths, the left one about an inch shorter than the other. This was a major contributing factor to her back problems. I have never been more amazed as I watched them pray for her and saw Holly's left leg lengthen in front of my eyes, only stopping when it reached the same length as the right. Wow! I wholeheartedly believe God heals today!

? What is your initial reaction to this story? Discuss it with a partner.

a Jess believes that she has seen a modern miracle.

Activities

1 Write two definitions of a miracle – one reflecting Jess' views and one Mr Arens'.

2 Imagine that you are the interviewer on a radio show, and that Jess is your special guest. Create the script for your discussion. Make sure that you include a range of possible interpretations of her story.

3 'If you are a Christian, you should believe in the reality of miracles. Without them, your faith means nothing.' Write a short response to this statement. Ensure that it's balanced and refers to the views of an Arens family member.

Raising Questions, Exploring Answers

Objectives

- Evaluate the contribution that Christianity can make to the life of an individual in the twenty-first century.
- Compare and contrast different Christian beliefs and attitudes to some ultimate questions.

Task

'Evil, suffering, tragedy and human failures present us with enormous challenges in life.'

Your task is to write or illustrate (on one A4 sheet of paper) your thoughts on how different Christians would try to respond to this statement. You should also include your own response.

A bit of guidance...

You can prepare for this task by thinking about the following questions: What answers would different Christians give in response to conflict, medical ethics, or any other topic from this unit? Where might they find it hard to provide an answer? How would you respond to these challenges?

In order to give a strong and complete answer, you need to present at least two different approaches (for example, two different Christian views) to the statement, with an explanation of which one you agree with more, and why.

Hints and tips

To help you tackle this task, you could look carefully at the units you have studied, particularly the case studies, to help you understand Christian responses to these issues. You could also read back over the work you've done in this chapter and decide how you think different Christians would respond to an issue:

- Would they be in agreement over certain things?
- What can a Christian use to help them address issues such as evil or conflict?
- What would you use?

Guidance

What level are you aiming at? Have a look at the grid below to see what you need to do to achieve that level. What would you need to do to improve your work?

I can...	
Level 3	• begin to identify the impact that Christianity has on a believer's life • ask important questions about Christianity and beliefs, making links between my own and others' responses.
Level 4	• describe the impact of Christianity on peoples' lives and show understanding of practices, beliefs and experiences • apply my ideas to my own life and the lives of others, describing what inspires and influences me and other people.
Level 5	• explain how Christian sources are used to provide answers to ultimate questions, recognizing the diversity of belief within Christianity • express my own and others' views on the challenges of belonging to a faith.
Level 6	• interpret teachings and explain reasons given by different Christian traditions to provide answers to ultimate questions • consider the challenges of belonging to a faith in the contemporary world, focussing on values and commitments.

Ready for more?

When you have completed this task, you can also work on your skills for Levels 6 and 7, and perhaps even higher. This is an extension task.

Your task is to write the **concluding** paragraph for an essay with the following claim:

'Christianity is increasingly irrelevant in this modern age.'

Imagine that you have already written the bulk of the essay. Consider the arguments that you would have included. You could first make a list of bullet points that show at least two different perspectives on the above statement, making sure that the points you make link into each other.

Learning Objectives

In this unit you will:

- learn why charity is important to Christians
- explain the meaning and role of sacrifice in giving
- discuss whether people are obliged to give to charity
- reflect on your own views about giving to charity.

Starter

- Have you ever raised any money for charity? Sport Relief? Local bake sale? Why or why not?
- Create a list of pros and cons about giving to charity.

In the Bible, Jesus gave some very challenging teachings about the use of money and giving to those in need. Each of the Bible passages to the right reveals a different angle on human attitudes to money. It could be argued that, according to these teachings, having money and following Jesus are incompatible. Some Christians give up all their wealth in order to serve those in need.

Other Christians interpret the teachings differently. They suggest that Christians can be wealthy, but shouldn't let money become their 'master'. They might argue that they cannot give to the poor if they have nothing to give in the first place.

'Truly I tell you, it is hard for someone who is rich to enter the kingdom of heaven. Again I tell you, it is easier for a camel to go through the eye of a needle than for someone who is rich to enter the kingdom of God.'
Matthew 19:23–24

'No one can serve two masters. Either you will hate the one and love the other, or you will be devoted to the one and despise the other. You cannot serve both God and money.'
Matthew 6:24

'Watch out! Be on your guard against all kinds of greed; life does not consist in an abundance of possessions.'
Luke 12:15

? J.K. Rowling gives a substantial amount of her money away to charity, yet is still very rich. Is giving truly giving if it doesn't involve sacrifice? Create a social networking post of 130–140 characters, considering some of the ideas and teachings on this page.

Case Study

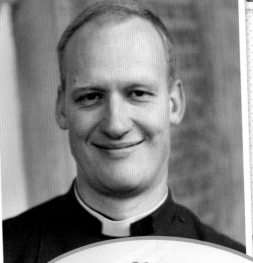

Mr and Mrs Arens give money regularly. They focus on giving to developing countries and to disadvantaged children. They also give a percentage of their income to the Church, because they believe that charity begins at home.

Mrs Arens views giving as a responsibility: 'Christians should help others and be charitable, because that is the commandment we were given: "Love each other as yourselves".'

However, she emphasizes the importance of giving wisely: 'Caring for others does not mean neglecting your own needs. It doesn't mean that you give yourself away, or drain yourself'. She refers to the teaching of Jesus: 'We are called to love ourselves as well'.

Mr Arens adds: 'God says that we are all extremely dear to him and we are called to show something of that to others. It's not always easy but that is what we are asked to do'.

? Look at the three Biblical passages on the opposite page. Which one do you think reflects what Mr and Mrs Arens are saying? What do you think they would say about the others?

Reflection

'Those who have plenty should give to those who have little.' Should all lottery winners be required to give a percentage of their winnings to charity?

Activities

1 What would a Christian say to someone who wants as much money as they can get, regardless of the consequences?

2 Many Christians give regularly, and not just money. In what other ways do you think someone could give that don't involve money? Create a 'Charity List'.

3 'Love your neighbour as you love yourself.' Christians aim to show love to others. Is showing love the same as giving charity?

4 'It doesn't matter what anyone says. It's still my money.' 'People need to learn to look after themselves and not live on handouts.' 'People give money just to make themselves feel better or look good.' Do you agree or disagree with these statements? Prepare your arguments and share your responses with a partner.

Learning Objectives

In this unit you will:

- learn what Christians believe about love and marriage
- understand how Christians see the role of God in a marriage
- evaluate the place of marriage, including same-sex marriage, in today's society.

Starter

- What happens at a wedding?
- Discuss with a partner what promises a couple should make when they get married.

Do love and marriage always go together? Many people believe they do and say that if two people love each other, they should get married. Others feel that love is enough, and marriage is no longer necessary.

Traditionally, Christians view that marriage as the lifelong union of a man and a woman (see quotations on this page). Many Christians share **vows** similar to these at a wedding ceremony:

Useful Words

Sacrament Signs of God's loving power in the world
Vow A promise or commitment

I [name] take you [name]
to be my wife/husband,
to have and to hold
from this day forward;
for better, for worse,
for richer, for poorer,
in sickness and in health,
to love and to cherish,
till death us do part;
In the presence of God I make this vow.

'*Marriage should be honoured by all.*'
Hebrews 13:4

'*But at the beginning of creation God made them male and female. For this reason a man will leave his father and mother and be united to his wife, and the two will become one flesh.*'
Mark 10:6–8

Christians believe that these marriage vows are made in God's presence and are, therefore, one of the most significant commitments in a person's life. Roman Catholics also believe that marriage is one of the seven **sacraments**, and is a special gift from God.

? Christians describe God as the 'third person' in the wedding ceremony. Why do you think this is, and why might this be important for Christians?

In 2004, civil partnerships were legalized in the UK. This meant that two people of the same gender could be joined together with the same legal status as in a marriage. Since then, there have been discussions about legalizing same-sex marriage, which would allow the ceremony to take place in church. There have been a number of different responses to this issue, both inside and outside different Christian Churches.

Tom French, policy co-ordinator for the Equality Network, said: 'Same-sex marriage is about equality and freedom – the freedom for couples to celebrate same-sex marriages, but equally, upholding the freedom of religious groups to say no to same-sex marriages.'

The Anglican Church said that same-sex marriages would: 'alter the intrinsic nature of marriage as the union of a man and a woman, as enshrined in human institutions throughout history.'

? Read all the quotations to the right carefully and then do a little research about the topic. Create a balanced range of responses and discuss with a partner what you think the decision should be about same-sex marriage. Explain your reasons.

Quakers in Britain stated: 'Quakers see God in everyone and that leads us to say that all committed loving relationships are of equal worth and so [we] wish to celebrate them in the same way.'

The above quotations represent just three of the varied views expressed about this issue. There are Christians on both sides of the debate. 2013 is the date proposed by the government for same-sex marriage to be legalized in England and Wales, but the Church of England and Church in Wales will be banned from offering such marriages. Other religious organizations have the choice to conduct same-sex marriages in their places of worship. As you can see, there will be many more debates about this issue over the next few years.

Reflection

'Love makes the world go round.' Do you agree? If not love, what else?

Activities

1 Look carefully at the marriage vows opposite. Are there any you would change or add? Rank them in order of importance. Explain your reasons.

2 Do you think that a vicar or priest should be required to marry a gay couple if they disagree with same-sex partnerships? What if the couple are practising Christians and members of the church? Discuss with a partner.

3 'Marriage is no longer an important part of modern society.' How would you respond to this?

5.3 Special Feature
What Makes a Family?

Learning Objectives

In this unit you will:

- consider some of the key Christian teachings about family
- evaluate the ways in which members of a family can support one another
- reflect on similarities and differences in modern families and identify what you believe is important for a family.

Starter

- Think about the TV programmes and films you watch. How many different families can you think of? Which are your favourite families and why?

During the last few decades, there have been many changes to the perception of what a family is thought to be – from the traditional mum, dad and two children, to single parents, half brothers and sisters, step-parents and siblings, same-gender parents and large community upbringing. There is no single way to define a family these days. Many people even look beyond their relatives to others who they class as family.

Jesus didn't get married, but he created his own extended family from the disciples and those around him. Because of Jesus' example, many Christians believe that whilst their relatives are a blessing to be treasured, the family of God is the most important.

'Then people brought little children to Jesus for him to place his hands on them and pray for them. But the disciples rebuked them. Jesus said, "Let the little children come to me, and do not hinder them, for the kingdom of heaven belongs to such as these."'
Matthew 19:13–14

'Someone told him, "Your mother and brothers are standing outside, wanting to speak to you." He replied, "Who is my mother, and who are my brothers?" Pointing to his disciples, he said, "Here are my mother and my brothers. For whoever does the will of my Father in heaven is my brother and sister and mother."'
Matthew 12:47–50

? Why do you think the disciples tried to stop people bringing children to Jesus? What was Jesus' response?

Many Christians believe that their immediate family should reflect the love that Jesus has for his people. There are teachings in the Bible that encourage husbands and wives to love one another, as well as passages telling parents to love their children and vice versa.

? Using the information in this unit, create a mind-map entitled 'The Christian family'. Try to refer to the Church, as well as immediate relatives and relevant Bible passages.

The Arens family believes that 'living in stable, loving relationships is important for everybody, especially for children growing up.' Mrs Arens says that it's important for adult relationships to be 'respectful and loving' too.

While family life is very important in many churches, Mr Arens says: 'Christians traditionally have affirmed that single life can be a very blessed thing for some people, and married life can be a very blessed thing for other people.'

The parents try to pass on their values to their children. Mrs Arens says: 'I hope that the way the children grow up with us has given them enough self-value, enough respect for others, that they will find loving relationships — whether with one partner for a lifetime, or with a circle of friends, or independent in themselves.'

Reflection

'A family can be created by any group of people prepared to show you love and respect.' How often do you receive love and respect, and give it to others?

Activities

1 In just one sentence, explain why the family is so significant for Christians.

2 In pairs or threes, create a series of short drama sketches that demonstrate what you think a family can give and encourage in one another.

3 Using the information in this unit, design a website homepage for a local church that encourages people to go and be part of the family of Jesus. Make it appealing for all ages and needs.

4 Mr and Mrs Arens hope that their children will grow up with self-value and respect for others. How might being part of a family help with this? In what situations might it not?

5 'For sale: the perfect parents and siblings.' What would they be like? Would you want them? Discuss why or why not with a partner.

Learning Objectives

In this unit you will:

- develop an understanding about why environmental issues are important for many Christians
- explain the meaning and significance of stewardship for Christians
- research and analyse views about what it means to be 'green'.

As the Muppet Kermit the Frog once said: 'It's not easy being green'. What does it mean to be 'green'? Nowadays, businesses provide everything fast – fast food, fast service, fast transport, even tourist trips to space! What these businesses don't always tell us is what had to be produced, consumed and destroyed in order to make all these things available.

Should we just ignore these issues and allow them to get worse, or should we take responsibility and act? Many Christians believe in the need to act. Christians believe that God created the Earth to be enjoyed and treasured. They also believe that humans were appointed by God to be stewards (see the quotation from Genesis), which means that they have a responsibility to look after and sustain the Earth.

Therefore, if asked the question: 'Is it important to be green?' a Christian might argue that it is – not only because they want to live sustainably, but because they want to serve God's creation.

'Then God said "Let us make mankind in our image, in our likeness, so that they may rule over the fish in the sea and the birds in the sky, over the livestock and all the wild animals, and over all the creatures that move along the ground."'
Genesis 1:26

'I brought you into a fertile land to eat its fruit and rich produce. But you came and defiled my land and made my inheritance detestable.'
Jeremiah 2:7

? Interview each other about green issues, in pairs or threes, and analyse your findings. Start by making a list of three questions asking for opinions about green issues, and then ask what three things each group member does that could be classed as 'green' (such as recycling or riding a bike instead of getting a lift).

Case Study

Quakers try to live their lives in accordance with Testimonies, or sets of values and principles relating to equality, simplicity, peace and truth. There is now discussion amongst Quakers about adding a fifth principle: sustainability.

For the White family, the belief that 'there is that of God' in everyone, applies directly to green issues. They aim to live a life that is simple, uncomplicated and **sustainable**. They don't want to live in a way that causes others to suffer because of a choice or an action that they might make.

Mr White not only believes in the idea of stewardship, but also that everyone is part of an ongoing 'creative process', which begins with God.

The Earth holds the resources that we have to use to contribute towards the creative process, but because it is an ongoing process we have to sustain this Earth. It is not ours to do what we like with. It is ours to use responsibly.

Reflection

'Thank God men cannot fly, and lay waste the sky as well as the earth.' Henry David Thoreau, nineteenth-century American philosopher. Much has changed since Thoreau's time. What might Thoreau say if he were alive today?

? Do you think it is worth doing small 'green' acts? Do you think they will make a difference?

Useful Words

Sustainable Does not run out or get used up

Activities

1. In your own words, define stewardship. Design a job profile for a steward.

2. Create a list of 'dos and don'ts' from God, as Creator, for how humanity should behave on Earth.

3. Design a board game that takes a player from 'no responsibility' through to 'stewardship'. What issues and questions could be included? What challenges would the players face?

4. 'I can't be bothered. I'm living life for me and for now. Why should I worry about future generations?'
   a How would you respond to this statement?
   b How would a Quaker respond to you?

5.5 How Fair is Fair?

Learning Objectives

In this unit you will:

- develop an understanding of what is meant by 'fair trade' and why it matters for Christians
- identify and evaluate different ways in which things can be fair trade.
- reflect on your own views about the importance of creating a fairer world.

Starter

- Create your own definition for the term, 'fair trade'.
- Should we worry about where the things we buy come from? Why or why not?

It's very easy to see the inequalities that exist in the world. A small percentage of people and companies owns a large percentage of the wealth. These people also control the prices paid for crops and other commodities. This means that, even if a poorer farmer is able to grow crops to sell, they are often unable to get a fair price for them.

Micah, an Old Testament prophet, asks what humans are expected to do, and the response is 'to act justly and to love mercy and to walk humbly with your God' (Micah 6:8). Christianity teaches that everybody is loved by God – and everyone should show mercy to their fellow humans – we all deserve to be treated fairly.

The Fairtrade Foundation was established in 1992 to try to achieve this. Some of the founding groups and other members are Christian groups that recognized the need for change. These include CAFOD (the Catholic Agency For Overseas Development), Christian Aid, Methodist Relief and Development Fund, and the United Reformed Church.

So what does Fairtrade do? The Foundation aims to ensure fair prices and decent living conditions for workers and their families in the developing world. It enables all those involved to have more control over improving their own lives, by helping to pay for things like healthcare and education for Fairtrade communities.

a The iconic Fairtrade logo is widely recognized.

b A Fairtrade farmer picking tea in Uganda.

72

Case Study

Katie Feller clarifies what she understands to be fair trade by pointing out that, if you buy a fair trade product, the people in the poor country that produced it are paid fairly. Some people have pointed out, though, that fair trade products are more expensive. Her mother explains why this is: 'By buying fair trade items you help poor people, because more money goes to the people who are actually doing the work.'

The Fellers go on to explain that it's not just about giving a fair price for a product, it goes deeper than that. As Katie puts it: 'Jesus said when he had the Last Supper [...] love one another as I have loved you, so that is why Christians want to give people the pay they deserve.'

c Selling local produce is very important to farmers' markets like this one.

Mr and Mrs Feller believe that fair trade can also be understood outside the Fairtrade Foundation. For them, it's just as important to give local UK producers a fair chance to sell their products through local farmers' markets, for example. The big supermarkets can provide everything, but they don't always support those around them.

Reflection

Where do you think the focus should be – on local producers who are losing customers in a more-developed country, or on producers unfairly treated in a less-developed country? Which would you support first?

Activities

1 Write a letter from a Fairtrade producer in a developing country to the Fairtrade Foundation, explaining the difference that membership has made to their business.

2 Go to the website of a supermarket and find five meals that could be made that include primarily Fairtrade products.

3 What would Jesus do? Look back at his teachings and create a selection of slogans for badges about fair trade that Jesus could have written.

Learning Objectives

In this unit you will:

- learn what is meant by multifaith and multiculture
- develop an understanding of how Christians see their role in a multifaith, multicultural society
- explore your own views and experiences of the society around you.

Starter

- Create a mind-map that includes all the faiths and cultures that you can think in your local area.

Britain today is a multifaith, multicultural society where people from many religions and backgrounds live alongside each other. Sometimes there are clashes between groups, which hit news headlines, but most people want to get on with each other.

It is possible for people who have different beliefs to work together, 'side by side', on shared projects, such as charity work, or campaigns for justice. It is also important for people to speak 'face to face' to learn more about each other.

A charity called Coexist works to promote unity and understanding between Christians, Jews and Muslims, but there has been a range of reactions from Christians to this type of **interfaith** organization. Some would argue that working too closely with other faiths might require Christians to compromise on the central importance of Jesus. They might argue that it's not possible for different faiths to have the same unified purpose.

Other Christians would argue that if they want to share the love of Jesus with someone, they must first be open to hearing and understanding what others believe.

? Do you think that it's fair to expect different religions to be open and accepting of each other? Discuss this with a partner.

The Christian Church often tries to encourage unity and many Christians believe in taking an **ecumenical** approach to Church. Organizations such as Churches Together in Britain and Ireland (CTBI) strive to be 'one in Christ'. They express this with the phrase: 'more together, less apart'.

> 'There is neither Jew nor Gentile, neither slave nor free, nor is there male and female, for you are all one in Christ Jesus.'
> Galatians 3:28

Reflection

'If all the faiths and cultures in this world worked alongside each other, what a different world it would be.' Do you agree? How might it be different? Do you think it could ever be achieved? Why or why not?

c Heads of many Christian denominations attend a meeting of prayer and reflection.

? Think back to your mind-map of faiths and cultures that you made at the start of this unit. Do you think you could see all of these groups working together with a common aim? Why or why not? What might the barriers be?

Useful Words

Ecumenical Promoting and working towards unity between Christian denominations
Interfaith Between faiths

Activities

1 What kind of society do you think we would have if everyone believed in the same thing? Write the first page of a novel that describes what this would be like.

2 **a** Do some research to find out about your local faith or interfaith group. Who is in it? What are their aims? What do they do?

b Prepare a list of questions to ask someone who belongs to that group.

3 What does 'coexist' mean? Design your own logo for the word. How many different symbols can you include?

4 Prepare a brief for an architect who is designing a new multifaith worship space for your school, or for the local hospital. What would you include in this space?

Christian Beliefs in Action

Objectives

- Evaluate some key questions and issues of the modern world and identify and analyse some different Christian responses to them.

- Develop key skills by preparing and arguing a case, and convincing others about one of the key issues.

Task

Your task is to design a campaign based on one of the issues raised in or linked to the units in this chapter. This can be done in groups or as individuals, depending on your teacher's instructions. Your campaign needs to have a goal or something to achieve. It will need to reflect not only your own and/or your group's opinions, but also your learning about the range of Christian beliefs expressed in this chapter.

A bit of guidance...

The information about this campaign needs to be produced using a form of ICT and will need to convince any reader or listener that what you are campaigning for deserves their attention — whether it's a demand for greater recycling, charity or multicultural awareness, for example. Your teacher will let you know if this is to be presented to the class or handed in as a completed assignment.

Hints and tips

To help you tackle this task, you could include the attitudes shown by Christians and non-Christians to the campaign issue of your choice, whether it be:

- giving to charity (money/time)
- traditional or same-sex marriage
- being green as a lifestyle choice
- embracing a multicultural and multifaith society
- or something else you have identified from this chapter.

Make sure you include references to relevant Christian teachings and to the views of the case study families.

Guidance

What level are you aiming at? Have a look at the grid below to see what you need to do to achieve that level. What would you need to do to improve your work?

	I can...
Level 3	• begin to identify the impact that Christianity has on a believer's life • ask important questions about Christianity and beliefs, making links between my own and others' responses.
Level 4	• describe the impact of Christianity on peoples' lives and show understanding of practices, beliefs and experiences • raise, and suggest answers to, questions about belonging, meaning, truth and commitment to a belief in God.
Level 5	• explain how Christian sources are used to provide answers to ultimate questions, and the impact of these sources on individuals • ask and suggest answers to questions of meaning, values and commitment, relating to my own and others' lives.
Level 6	• explain why the impact of Christianity and beliefs on individuals and communities can vary • use reasoning and examples to express insights into the relationship between beliefs, teachings and world issues.

Ready for more?

When you have completed this task, you can also work on your skills for Levels 6 and 7, and perhaps even higher. This is an extension task.

Look at the issues listed on the opposite page under 'Hints and tips'. You need to decide which one you think is the most pressing and relevant issue for you, as if it's your own mini campaign.

In order to do this, choose the three issues that you think are most significant and identify their strengths and weaknesses. This could be: 'Relevant to a large number of people'. or 'Difficult for some, because money is a problem'. It's important that you have both the strengths **and** the weaknesses to be testing your skills at Level 7.

Create one paragraph for each issue using these evaluations and then choose the issue that you think has the most strengths.

Glossary

Abortion Medically removing a baby from the womb during pregnancy

Anglican Part of the Church of England, the official Church of the country, with the Queen as the head

Archbishop A chief bishop responsible for a large area of the UK

Baptism, Believer's A ceremony for adults or teenagers, involving water, which symbolizes the start of their new spiritual life

Baptism, Infant A ritual that welcomes a young child into the Christian Church

Baptist A member of a Christian denomination that practises adult baptism

Big Bang A scientific theory that suggests the universe was created billions of years ago by an explosion of dense matter, which gradually expanded to form planets, stars – and eventually life itself, including humans

Civil Rights Movement A movement that fought for the rights of all people, regardless of their skin colour

Conception The moment that a sperm cell fertilizes an egg and a woman becomes pregnant

Confirmation A Christian ceremony during which a teenager or adult affirms their Christian belief

Congregation Members of the church

Conscientious objectors Those who refuse to fight on the grounds of religious beliefs or conscience

Controversial Likely to be opposed by many people

Crucifix The figure of Jesus nailed to a cross

Crucifixion A Roman method of execution that involved nailing a person to a large wooden cross until they died

Denomination Families of Churches, such as Catholic, Anglican and Pentecostal

Disciples Followers; Jesus had many disciples who he taught and lived among

Ecumenical Promoting and working towards unity between Christian denominations

Eucharist The meal of bread and wine that Christians share together to remember the death and resurrection of Jesus

First Holy Communion A sacrament of the Roman Catholic Church, during which a young person first receives the Eucharist

Foetus The name given to a developing human in pregnancy

Free Church A church that is independent of any official denomination

Free will Having the freedom to choose what to do

Gospel 'Good news'; the 'Gospels' are the four books at the start of the New Testament in the Bible, and contain the life and teachings of Jesus

Grace God's love and blessing, given to all, even if they haven't earned it

Hail Mary A prayer to Mary the mother of Jesus, praising her and asking for her help

Holy Spirit The Spirit of God

Holy Trinity God in three persons: Father, Son and Holy Spirit

Immanent God is present within his creation and his people

Incarnation The embodiment of God the Son in human form as Jesus Christ

Interfaith Between faiths

Just war The belief that wars can be morally justified if they meet certain criteria

Mass The most important act of worship during which Roman Catholics and some Anglicans believe they receive Christ through bread and wine

Minister An ordained member of the Church

Miracles Amazing events believed to be caused by God

Monotheism Belief in one God

New Testament collection of books and letters forming the second part of the Christian Bible

Old Testament Collection of books forming the first part of the Christian Bible, which is shared with Judaism

Original Sin A common Christian belief that all humans are born sinful as a result of Adam and Eve disobeying God

Pacifist A person who believes in non-violent solutions to conflict

Passover A Jewish festival celebrating the escape of the Jews from slavery

Pentecost Originally a Jewish harvest festival; also the Christian celebration of the coming of the Holy Spirit to the disciples

Pentecostal churches Churches that have separated from the Roman Catholic Church and believe in the dramatic workings of the Holy Spirit

Priest An ordained person who leads a Christian community

Purgatory Mostly a Roman Catholic belief; a place or process where people who have died are healed fully (from their sins) before experiencing God in heaven

Quakers Members of the Religious Society of Friends established by George Fox in the seventeenth century

Resurrection The Christian belief that God raised Jesus from the dead on the third day after his crucifixion

Rite A ritual or ceremony that represents something

Ritual Something done repeatedly and regularly in the same or similar format each time

Roman Catholicism Holds the Pope as the Head of the Church and performs Mass and other sacraments

Rosary A string of beads with a cross, used in prayer and meditation

Sacrament Signs of God's loving power in the world

Sacred Holy, unique

Sacred Heart A painting of Jesus showing his human heart, which symbolizes his love for humanity

Salvation Being saved from something; in Christianity, deliverance from sin and its consequences

Satan In Christian belief, a supernatural person (or force) of evil in the world

Saviour A person or being who saves

Secular Without religious reference; non-religious

Segregation Legal and physical separation between black people and white people, especially in the southern USA up to the late 1960s

Sermon/homily A talk given during a church service about a Bible passage or religious theme

Sin Things that people think, do, or don't do that go against what God wants

Soul The non-physical part of a person; many Christians believe that is has a spiritual element

Sustainable Does not run out or get used up

Tax collectors People who collect money for the Government (in Jesus' time, tax collectors were known for being corrupt)

Theodicy A theory that explains how God and evil coexist

Tongues A special language given by the Holy Spirit

Vow A promise or commitment

Worship Any act that shows the devotion of the believer to God

Index